I AM

THE I AM BOOK

Compiled by
SUSAN EAVES

*Good Fellas Publishing
Osprey, FL 34229
GoodFellasoftheBible.com*

Copyright © 1989 by Susan Eaves
After 19 printings, second edition copyright © 2011 by Susan Eaves

Good Fellas Publishing
P.O. Box 7
Osprey, FL 34229
GoodFellasoftheBible.com

ISBN: 978-0-578-07695-9

All rights reserved. No part of this publication may be reproduced, stored in a retrieval system or transmitted, in any form, or by any means, electronic, mechanical, recorded, photocopied, or otherwise, without the prior written permission of both the copyright owner and the above publisher of this book, except by a reviewer who may quote brief passages in a review.

The scanning, uploading, and distribution of this book via the Internet or via any other means without the permission of the publisher is illegal and punishable by law. Please purchase only authorized electronic editions and do not participate on or encourage electronic piracy of copyrightable materials. Your support of the author's rights is appreciated.

All scriptures taken from King James version of the Bible unless otherwise indicated by NIV trademark of the New International Version of the Bible. Scriptures followed by NIV are taken from the Holy Bible, New International Version, copyright 1973, 1978, 1984 by International Bible Society.

Printed in the United States of America

Contents

SPECIAL ACKNOWLEDGEMENTS 9
DEDICATION 10
INTRODUCTION 11
HOW TO USE THIS BOOK 15
SIGN YOURSELF INTO GOD'S INTENSIVE CARE UNIT .. 17
DO YOU KNOW HIM? 20
IN CHRIST I AM… 22

SECTION I: WHO GOD IS 25
GOD IS 27
THE LORD IS 30
THE LOVE OF THE FATHER 32
THE LOVE OF THE HOLY SPIRIT 34
THE LOVE OF JESUS 35
THE BURDEN BEARER 37
GOD'S PLEASURE 39
AVENGER OF HIS ELECT 41
BUT GOD… 43
FATHER TO THE FATHERLESS 46
THE GOODNESS OF GOD 48
GOD'S THOUGHTS 50
THE COMFORTER 52
THE RESTORER 54
THE HELPER 56
THE GOD WHO LISTENS 58
THE FACE OF THE LORD 60
THE GOD OF PATIENCE AND CONSOLATION 61
THE WORD 63

GOD KNOWS YOU	66
THE DELIVERER	67
PRESERVER OF MEN	69
THE GOD OF TRUTH	71
THE WAY MAKER	73
THE HAND OF THE LORD	75
THOU	78
THE HUSBAND TO THE WIDOW	80
THE NAME OF THE LORD	83
THE GOD OF MERCY	85
REVEALER OF SECRETS	87
THE EYES OF THE LORD	89
OUR INHERITANCE	91
IN THE SHADOW OF HIS WINGS	93
HEALER OF THE BROKENHEARTED	95
THE GOD OF FAVOR	96
WHAT GOD DESIRES	98
HEALER OF THE SOUL	100
CONQUEROR OF SIN	101
BONDAGE BREAKER	103
HIS NAME IS JEALOUS	104
THE LIFTER OF MY HEAD	105
THE GOD OF HOPE	106
GOD KNOWS YOU	108
THE GOD WHO FORGIVES	109
GOD'S GENTLENESS	111
GOD ANSWERS PRAYER	112
THE ARM OF THE LORD	114
STRENGTH IN THE TIME OF TROUBLE	116
GOD'S IFS	118
GOD'S FAITHFULNESS	120
A FRIEND THAT LOVES AT ALL TIMES	122
FAITHFUL AND TRUE	124
THE LIGHT	125
THE PROMISE KEEPER	127
THE SERVANT	129

THE FOUNTAIN OF LIFE	131
THE VOICE OF THE LORD	133
GOD IS A GIFT GIVER	136
WHAT THE LORD HATES	137
I WILL	139
THE RIVER OF LIFE	144
THE PRINCE OF PEACE	146
THE RESCUER	148
THE GOD OF LIFE	150
SECTION II: THE HOLY SPIRIT	151
THE SPIRIT	153
THE HOLY SPIRIT LIVES IN US	155
DIRECTS	156
HE IS THE SPIRIT OF ADOPTION	157
GIVES POWER	158
BRINGS JOY	159
HE IS THE SPIRIT OF TRUTH	160
COMFORTS	161
GUIDES	162
TEACHES	163
HE BRINGS LIFE	164
HE SHOWS THINGS TO COME	165
HELPS OVERCOME WEAKNESSES	166
HE BRINGS FREEDOM	167
HE CAN BE GRIEVED	168
HE BEARS WITNESS	169
GIFTS OF THE HOLY SPIRIT	170
BLASPHEMING THE HOLY SPIRIT	171

SECTION III: WHAT YOU HAVE IN CHRIST 173
GIFTS OF THE SON 174
I AM 175
IN THE LORD 178
IN WHOM 180
THROUGH HIS BLOOD 182
IN THE NAME OF JESUS 184
BY HIM 186
WITH CHRIST 187
THROUGH CHRIST 188
THE FEAR OF THE LORD 189
THE COMPASSION OF JESUS 191
GODS GUIDANCE 193
CHRIST'S RIGHTEOUSNESS 194
BLESSINGS OF THE FEAR OF THE LORD 196
THROUGH HIM 198
WITH HIM 199
IN HIM 201
IN CHRIST JESUS 204

SECTION IV: HEALING 209
GOD'S THOUGHTS CONCERNING HEALING 210

SECTION V: TO BE BORN AGAIN 217
THE POWER OF THE CROSS 218
WHAT GOD WANTS YOU TO RECEIVE 220
TO BE BORN AGAIN 224

SUSAN EAVES 225

Special Acknowledgements

This project became a reality with the help of many. Special thanks to Anthony Sands who became my hands on this project. Special thanks to his children who sacrificed time with Dad to finish this project. Thank you to Jo Hoch, this would not have happened without your sacrificial giving of time and effort. Crystal Booth with your additional typing help. Joanne Derstine who edited the Introduction and How to Use This Book sections. Chris and Chuck Berster who took frantic phone calls from their technically challenged friend. Leta Perry who stepped in at the last minute to do the final editing. To my women's Bible study group who helped me with their prayers and encouragement. Thank you to my daughter Genesis who uplifted my spirit with such kind words.
Thanks to Kathy and Mary Ann for their prayer support.
You are the heroes that made this publication possible!

Dedication

This book is dedicated to you the reader. It is my prayer that you will come to know Jesus in such a deep and personal way, that all the people you touch will see the Master working in your life. May you find peace and joy in a greater measure than you have ever known.

> Love Eternal,
> Susan Eaves

Introduction

To the Fourth Edition of The I Am Book

I've been blessed to hear from many people telling me what a godsend ***The I Am Book*** has been in their lives. Thank you! Several have asked what inspired me to write this book. In answering that question, I must reveal one of my greatest struggles. I believe God wants me to share this very personal experience so that you, also, can find hope and help in God's word.

Almost thirty years ago I found myself on the front row of my church trying desperately not to scream. A voice inside my head was telling me, ***This is it. You're finally gonna have the nervous breakdown that you knew was coming. Scream, you know you can't control it anymore, just scream***. I was in a full-blown panic attack.

My whole body was shaking with fear and a torrent of uncontrollable tears streamed down my face. The church service hadn't started. Seated between two friends, I struggled to get words out of my mouth. "I think I'm having a nervous breakdown, I feel like I'm going to start screaming!"

"You're not going to have a breakdown," my friends said, trying to reassure me. "Just come to the back of the church with us and we'll pray for you in one of the offices." Feeling intense humiliation and then horror, I replied, "I can't move. I don't remember how to walk." I was going to pieces before the entire church and fighting for my sanity at the same time.

My wonderful friends gently lifted me out of my seat, and coaxed me down the aisle. Although they were right next to me, their voices seemed far away. "There you go, Susan, put your left foot down, good Susan, now put your right foot down." The other church members stared at the crazy woman having a meltdown. It was surreal. It seemed like everything was happening in excruitiatingly slow motion as I labored to walk past a sea of baffled people whose eyes were fixed on me.

My friends prayed for me and it did pass. I didn't have a nervous breakdown that night. Still, I was beside myself with humiliation and helplessness. Internally, I berated myself. ***You have to stop doing this! Why can't you control yourself like other people?***

I suffered panic attacks from the time I was a little girl, although I didn't tell anyone what was happening. Unfortunately, our family had a lot of "secrets". We didn't talk openly about our problems or what was bothering us. I just made excuses when I felt overwhelmed by panic. I'd say, "I'm not feeling good," or make some other feeble excuse. The truth was I didn't know what was going on or why it was happening.

After the major meltdown at my church, I kept asking God, "What is wrong with me? Why does this continue to happen to me?" I considered myself a complete failure. I had two degrees in education and had taught everything from first grade through college, yet I was unable to prevent or stop the panic attacks. I never knew when the next one would hit. Many times the panic attacks would happen in the grocery store and I would leave a cart of groceries in the aisle and run so I wouldn't start screaming.

Inwardly, I felt God prompting me to study His Word and get to know Him. So I began to search the Bible on God's character. What pleased Him? How could I recognize His voice? I had heard many opinions of others telling me what God was like, but I didn't know for myself what the Bible said about Him. While growing up, anytime something horrible happened to us we were told, "God is mad at you. This happened because He is punishing you." It's hard to have faith in a God that you believe is always angry with you and "out to get ya".

Through my study of His Word, I found out that He wasn't "out to get me". The truth has power. The truth was that He wanted to chase me down with His love, and pour out His peace, joy and blessings on me. I had believed lies long enough. The truth was setting me free!

I started writing down the names and titles of God. One of His titles was **The Prince of Peace** and reading that name gave me peace. Another title was the **God of all Comfort;** I would walk with my index cards saying to myself, **The God of all Comfort is comforting me.** Still, another said, He is **The God of Mercy.** How wonderful it was to know to that God wasn't mad at me! I could count on Him to show me mercy. I carried those names around with me on index cards in my purse. Whenever I felt panic-stricken I would get out my cards and read. I would say to myself, **The Prince of Peace is with me or The Way Maker will make a way for me.**

Many times I would feel His presence. At other times, I would start to feel more peaceful and comforted. I didn't always experience immediate help, but gradually the attacks became less and less until they eventually didn't happen at all. I was free. What life and joy that freedom brought me! Getting to know God made all the difference.

People at my church noticed such a change in me they asked for my notes on God's character. I was thrilled to copy them and gave them out to all who asked. I couldn't believe such liberty and freedom had been available to me all along. I never experienced it because I never studied the Bible to know Him.

I continued my research and it eventually became a book. So many people said getting to know God revolutionized their lives. I heard from people who suffered with anxiety and addictions. Entire AA groups would order my little book. It has been such a privilege to hear the life changing transformations that took place.

God took my greatest place of defeat and humiliation and turned it into a miracle for me and so many others. I believe He wants to do the same in your life. I never did have that nervous breakdown, I now pray for people with all types of problems. Yes, I still have problems but I am no longer without hope.

I know the Source of all Hope and so can you. Please read on and know you're not alone. It was not an accident that you opened up this book. God longs to help you. Another one of His titles is that He is *The Helper.* I can assure you by the authority of His Word, that He will help you through any and every trial and crisis. He is *Faithful.* You can count of Him. He is *The Friend that Loves at All Times.* He can be trusted with all of your cares and concerns.

I have taken Him at His word. He's come through time and time again when things looked hopeless or beyond repair. Millions of desperate people throughout the centuries have proven His Word as true. No wonder the Bible is still the best-selling book of all time. It is a book of supernatural provision for every area of your life. **God's words are alive and have the power to change any life, including yours!**

How to Use this Book

If you are using this book to help you overcome some type of addiction, bad habit or panic attacks, I would like to encourage you that God is with you every step of the way on your journey to wholeness. If you are overwhelmed and can no longer function effectively I urge you to see a medical professional. At times in my own life, doctors have been an answer to prayer. I only allow doctors into my life that have a positive outlook on my prognosis. At this point of my journey I am overcoming a neurological disease that there is no known cure for. I had to go through many doctors before I found one that told me, "Don't write hope out of the equation." His words gave me life and hope. Although my diagnosis is serious, it's not terminal. I believe The God of Miracles has a miracle for me.

If I had a disease that I was told was terminal, I would seek the best medical care I could find and I would continue to believe in a miracle- working Jesus.

I would read the scriptures written in this book every day. I would read The I Am Book several times a day, one page or verse at a time. I would say the verses aloud and personalize them with my name in those verses. Jesus said, "With God all things are possible", I believe with God the impossible becomes possible.

I would watch Christian television, and listen to Christian radio as well as view positive Christian based programs on the internet. I would not allow negative friends, family or associates to tear down my faith. I am very careful to share my beliefs concerning a miracle in my life with those of like faith. Jesus said, "Don't cast your pearls before swine". Scripture verses are precious pearls God gives to those who believe. Don't share them with mockers.

I would also carefully monitor the music and television

I am watching. If you are dealing with panic attacks, don't watch horror or heart pounding programs. If you are dealing with physical sickness, don't watch medical shows that show people dying from disease and trauma. Create an atmosphere for miracles.

If you have addictions, don't view shows that glamorize drugs and alcohol. Don't listen to music that glorifies the drug lifestyle. God will do His part, but He requires His children to do theirs. What you are unable to do, God will give you the grace to do.

Sign Yourself into God's Intensive Care Unit

What would happen to you if you were in the Intensive Care unit in a hospital? All of the medical attention would be focused on getting you well. The hospital staff would monitor your communication. They would limit who was allowed in your room. Extra diligence would be made to keep your environment germ and virus free. No loud, blaring music or emotionally unstable people would be allowed in. You would be given foods and medicines that would make you strong and healthy again. God's Word is medicine and food for your body and soul; **take God's Word as if your life depended upon it, because it does!**

A checklist of things to bring us into God's Intensive Care unit:

- First - shut everything down, limit phone calls or eliminate unnecessary calls altogether.

- Read the Word several times a day. Pray and ask God to open up your understanding and give you wisdom for your situation.

- At work, copy scriptures that minister to you. Read them aloud with your name in it. In other words -"I will do all things through Christ who strengthens me", or "God always cause me to triumph in Christ Jesus".

- Use one of God's titles - Jesus said, "When I go I will send the Comforter to you, you will not be alone". Say aloud softly, if at work, "The Comforter is with me. He is comforting me and strengthening me. I will triumph over this situation!" Or you might say, "The Advocate is on my side. He is giving me favor fighting for me in this situation."

- Don't watch the news before bed.

- Play positive and uplifting music.

- Watch what your mouth is saying. If you are constantly repeating, "I'm a nervous wreck" or "I'll never get well" your body will *move* in that direction. What if I don't recover? ***What if you do?***

- Think about all the things you want to do when you are well. Plan your future, healed and whole.

- Before you fall asleep at night see yourself well or taking part in an activity you can't do presently.

You may ask, "Are you saying nothing bad will happen to me if I just believe?" I am not saying that. My own, precious twenty-one year old son went to heaven way before I would have liked him to. Of course, I wanted to give up. I went through the dark valley of the shadow of death. It was *hard,* but I chose to move forward and make new memories. Was it difficult? It was the toughest thing I've ever done, there were days that I wanted to just lay on the floor and scream. Every day I had to choose to continue moving forward. Was it worth the pain and effort? Yes, a thousand times yes!

Life is a precious gift from God. No matter how dark and hopeless things may appear, God will always make a way. You may be asking, "What if I'm terminal and I make these changes and I still die?" You will not have wasted your time! You would have invested your time in getting to know your Creator better and that's never a waste of time. There are eternal benefits to knowing God.

People spend so much time planning their retirements and vacations. So few stop to think where they are going to spend eternity. If you don't feel that you know Him personally, turn to the back of the book where it tells you how to be born again.

God bless you in your journey. He will give your life meaning and purpose. Don't wait another day to make Jesus the Lord of you life or to just get to know Him better. No one will ever love you more than He does! I'm looking forward to hearing about your answers to prayer.

With much love,
Susan

DO YOU KNOW HIM?

Jer 9:24 ▌ Let him that glorieth glory in this, that he understandeth and knoweth me, that I am the Lord which exercise lovingkindness, judgment, and righteousness, in the earth: for these things I delight, saith the Lord.

Jer 1:5 ▌ He is the One who knew you from your mother's womb.

Jer 1:19 ▌ He is the God who is with you to deliver you from your enemies.

Jer 2:9 ▌ He is the God who pleads with his people and priests "come back to me!"

Jer 3:15 ▌ He is the God who feeds his people with knowledge and understanding.

Jer 8:21 ▌ He is the God who hurts when his children hurt.

Jer 15:16 ▌ He is the Word unto you, the joy and rejoicing of your heart.

Jer 17:13 ▌ He is the fountain of living waters to the dry and thirsty soul.

Jer 17:17 ▌ He is my hope in the day of evil.

Jer 20:9 ▌ He is the Word burning in my heart as fire in my bones.

Jer 20:11 ▌ He is the mighty terrible one dealing with my persecutors.

Jer 18:4 ▌ He is the Potter forming you into a vessel fit for the Master's use.

Jer 23:16 ▌ I can come boldly before the throne of grace because he is the Lord my righteousness.

Jer 23:23 ▌ He is the God close at hand.

Jer 30:16 ▌ He is the Restorer of our health, the Healer of our wounds.

Jer 31:3 ▌ He is the Everlasting Love, - the Love of your life.

Jer 33:3 ▌ He is the God who answers when I call and shows me great and mighty things which I know not.

Jer 49:11 ▌ He is the Defender of the fatherless and the Husband to the widow.

Jer 50:34 ▌ He is the God who gives rest to his people.

Jer 51:5 ▌ He is the God who does not forsake his people even though they have sinned against him.

IN CHRIST I AM...

Phil 1:6 ▌ "That the communication of the faith may become effectual by the acknowledging of every good thing which is in you in Christ Jesus."

Be in agreement with God's Word. Let the words of your mouth say what He says about you!

In Christ I am-

I am born of God. 1 Jn 5:18.

I am led by the Spirit of the Living God. Rom 8:14

I am a temple of the Holy Spirit. 1 Cor 6:19

I am not my own. 1 Cor 6:19

I am bought with a price. 1 Cor 7:23

I am full of the love of God. Rom 5:5

I am forgiven. Col 1:14

I am walking in love. Eph 5:2

I am at peace with God through my Lord Jesus Christ. Rom 5:1

I am fully persuaded what he has promised, He is able and willing to do. Rom 4:21

I am not under the law, but under grace. Rom 6:16

I am free from the law of sin and death. Rom 8:2

I am walking in newness of spirit. Rom 7:6

I am giving my Father joy because I am walking in truth. 1 Jn 1:4

I am worth the body and blood of Jesus. Luke 22:18-19

I am receiving the unconditional love of God. Rom 5:8

I am seated in heavenly places in Christ Jesus. Eph 2:6

I am a saint. Eph 1:1

I am accepted. Eph 1:6

I am greatly loved. Dan 10:19

I am precious in the sight of the Lord. Ps 116:15

I am a servant. Ps 116:16

I am listened to by God my Father. Ps 116:1

I am dead to sin. Rom 6:11

I am alive unto God through Jesus Christ my Lord. Rom 6:11

I am free from condemnation. Rom 8:1

I am giving thanks in all things. Phil 4:6

I am laying aside all malice, envy and evil speaking. 1 Pet 2:1

I am partaking of God's divine nature. 2 Pet 1:4

I am not a victim, but an overcomer. Rev 12:11

I am fashioned by the Master's hand. Eph 2:10

I am of value to God. Matt 10:31

I am walking in great peace, because 1 love God's law (of love) and nothing does offend me. Ps 119:165

I am predestined to be conformed to the image of His Son. Rom 8:29

I am an overcomer by the Blood of the Lamb and the word of my testimony. Rom 12:11

I am wise in heart. Pro 10:8

I am healed by His stripes. Isa 53:5

I am strong in the Lord and the power of His might. Eph 6:10

I am speaking with the tongue of the learned. Isa 50:4.

I am not confounded because the Greater One lives in me. Isa 50:7, Jn 4:4

Section I

WHO GOD IS

GOD IS

God is MY HOPE. Rom 15:13

God is LOVE. 1 Jn 4:16

God is MY DELIVERER. Ps 18:2

God is MY STRENGTH. Ps 18:2

God is MY REFUGE. Ps 46:1

God is MIGHTY. Zeph 3:17

God is GRACIOUS and MERCIFUL 2 Chr. 30:9

God is HOLY. Ps 99:9

God is MY ROCK. Ps 42:9

God is MY EXCEEDING JOY. Ps 43:4

God is a SUN and a SHIELD. Ps 84:11

God is FAITHFUL. 1 Cor 10:13

God is LIGHT. 1 Jn 1:5

God is FOR ME. Ps 56:9

God is WITH ME IN ALL THAT I DO. Gen 21:22

God is MY DEFENSE. Ps 59:9

God is MY HELPER. Ps 54:4

God is MY SALVATION. Isa 12:2

God is RICH IN MERCY. Eph 2:4

God is WISER THAN MEN. 1 Cor 1:25

God is STRONGER THAN MEN. 1 Cor 1:25

God is not the author of confusion, but of PEACE. 1 Cor 14:33

God is a CONSUMING FIRE. Heb 12:29

God is GREATLY TO BE FEARED in the assembly of saints, to be had in reverence those that are about Him. Ps 89:7

God is not a man, that He should lie. Has He said and shall He not do it? Has He spoken and shall He not make it good? Num 23:19

God is not unrighteous to forget your work and labor of love. Heb 6:10

God is a VERY PRESENT HELP in trouble. Ps 46:1

God is GREATER THAN MY HEART, and He knows all things. 1 Jn 3:20

God is angry with the wicked every day. Ps 7:11

God is a Spirit, those that worship Him must worship Him in spirit and in truth. Jn 4:24

God is GOOD TO ISRAEL, and to such as are of a clean heart. Ps 73:1

God is a JEALOUS GOD. Deut 6:15

God is He that goes with you, to fight for you against your enemies. Deut 20:4

God is my STRENGTH AND POWER, He makes my way perfect. 2 Sam 22:33

God is RIGHTEOUS in all His works. Dan 9:14

God is not the God of the dead, but of the living. Matt 22:32

God is TRUE. Jn 3:33

God is NO RESPECTER OF PERSONS. Acts 10:34

God is ABLE to make all grace abound toward you. 2 Cor 9:8

God is NOT MOCKED; whatever a man sows he will reap. Gal 6:7

THE LORD IS

The Lord is MY ROCK. Ps 18:2

The Lord is GOOD. Nah 1:7

The Lord is a REFUGE FOR THE OPPRESSED. Ps 9:9

The Lord is a SRONGHOLD IN THE DAY OF TROUBLE. Nah 1:7

The Lord is my LIGHT. Ps 27:1

The Lord is my SALVATION. Ps 27:1

The Lord is my FORTRESS. Ps 18:2

The Lord is with them that uphold my soul. Ps 54:4

The Lord is POWERFUL. Ps 29:4

The Lord is FULL OF MAJESTY. Ps 29:4

The Lord is MY DEFENSE. Ps 89:18

The Lord is MERCIFUL, GRACIOUS, SLOW TO ANGER AND PLENTEOUS IN MERCY. Ps 103:8

The Lord is my KEEPER. Ps 121:5

The Lord is my HELPER, I will not fear what man can do to me. Heb 13:6

The Lord is the STRENGTH OF MY LIFE, of whom shall I be afraid? Ps 27:1

The Lord is FAITHFUL, He shall establish me and keep me from evil. 2 Thess 3:3

The Lord is RISEN INDEED. Luke 24:34

The Lord is VERY PITIFUL, and of TENDER MERCY. James 5:11

The Lord is GRACIOUS. 1 Pet 2:3

The Lord is against them that do evil. 1 Pet 3:12

The Lord is LONGSUFFERING. 2 Pet 3:9

The Lord is a GOD OF JUDGMENT. Isa. 30:18

The Lord is my STRENGTH and my REDEEMER. Ps 19:14.

The Lord is my SHEPHERD, I shall not want, Ps 23:1

The Lord is a MAN OF WAR. Ex 15:3.

The Lord is a MIGHTY WARRIOR. Jer 20:11

The Lord is my DELIVERER. 2 Sam 22:2

THE LOVE OF THE FATHER

Jn 16:27 ▌ For the FATHER HIMSELF LOVETH YOU, because ye have loved me, and have believed that I came out from God.

Isa 38:17 ▌ Behold, for peace I had great bitterness: but THOU HAST IN LOVE to my soul delivered it from the pit of corruption: for thou hast cast all my sins behind thy back.

Rom 5:8 ▌ But GOD COMMENDETH HIS LOVE toward us, in that, while we were yet sinners, Christ died for us.

Ps 42:8 ▌ Yet the LORD WILL COMMAND HIS LOVINGKINDNESS in the daytime, and in the night his song shall be with me, and my prayer unto the God of my life.

Eph 2:4 ▌ But God, who is rich in mercy, for his GREAT LOVE wherewith HE LOVED US.

Jn 14:21 ▌ He that hath my commandments, and keepeth them, he it is that loveth me: and he that loveth me SHALL BE LOVED OF MY FATHER, and I will love him, and will manifest myself to him.

1 Jn 4:19 ▌ We love him, because HE FIRST LOVED US.

1 Jn 4:9.10 ▌ In this was manifested the love of God toward us, because that God sent his only begotten Son into the world, that we might live through him. Herein is love, not that we loved God, but that HE LOVED US, and sent his Son to be the propitiation for our sins.

Jn 3:16 ▌ For GOD SO LOVED THE WORLD, that he gave his only begotten Son, that whosoever believed in him should not perish but have everlasting life.

1 Jn 3:1 ▍ Behold, WHAT MANNER OF LOVE THE FATHER HATH BESTOWED upon us, that we should be called the sons of GOD therefore the world knoweth us not, because it knew him not.

1 Jn 4:11 ▍ Beloved, if GOD SO LOVED US, we ought also to love one another.

1 Jn 4:16 ▍ And we have known and believed the LOVE THAT GOD HATH FOR US. God is love; and he that dwelleth in love dwelleth in God and God in him.

Deut 7:8 ▍ But because the LORD LOVED YOU, and because he would keep the oath which He had sworn unto your fathers, hath the Lord brought you out with a mighty hand, and redeemed you out of house of bondmen, from the hand of Pharaoh king of Egypt.

Jer 31:3 ▍ The Lord hath appeared of old unto me, saying, Yea, I HAVE LOVED THEE WITH AN EVERLASTING LOVE: therefore with lovingkindness have I drawn thee.

THE LOVE OF
THE HOLY SPIRIT

Rom 15:30 ▍ Now I beseech you, brethren, for the Lord Jesus Christ's sake, and for the LOVE OF THE SPIRIT, that ye strive together with-me in your prayers to God for me.

Rom 5:5 ▍ And hope maketh not ashamed; because the LOVE OF GOD is shed abroad in our hearts BY THE HOLY GHOST which is given unto us.

THE LOVE OF JESUS

1 Jn 3:16 ❚ Hereby perceive we the love of God, because he laid down his life for us: and we ought to lay down our lives for the brethren.

Jn 13:1 ❚ Now before the feast of the Passover, when Jesus knew that his hour was come that he should depart out of this world unto the Father, having LOVED HIS OWN which were in the world, he loved them unto the end.

Jn 15:13 ❚ GREATER LOVE HATH NO MAN than this, that a man lay down his life for his friends.

Rom 8:35 ❚ Who shall separate us from the LOVE OF CHRIST? shall tribulation, or distress, or persecution, or famine, or nakedness, or peril, or sword?

Jn 15:9 ❚ As the Father hath loved me, so have I LOVED YOU: continue ye in my love.

Eph 5:2 ❚ And walk in love, as CHRIST also hath LOVED US, and hath given himself for us an offering and a sacrifice to God for a sweet smelling savour.

Eph 3:17-19 ❚ That Christ may dwell in your hearts by faith; that ye, being rooted and grounded in love, may be able to comprehend with all saints what is the breadth, and length, and depth, and height; and to know the LOVE OF CHRIST, which passeth knowledge, that ye might be filled with all the fulness of God.

Rev 1:5 ▮ And from Jesus Christ, Who is the faithful witness, and the first begotten of the dead, and the prince of the kings of the earth. Unto HIM THAT LOVED US, and washed us from our sins in his own blood.

Rom 8:37 ▮ Nay, in all these things we are more than conquerors through HIM THAT LOVED US.

Jn 14:21 ▮ He that hath my commandments, and keepeth them, he it is that loveth me: and he that loveth me shall be loved of my Father, and I WILL LOVE HIM, and will manifest myself to him.

Titus 3:3-4 ▮ For we ourselves also were sometimes foolish, disobedient, deceived, serving divers lusts and pleasures, living in malice and envy, hateful, and hating one another. But after that the kindness and LOVE OF GOD OUR SAVIOUR toward man appeared.

THE BURDEN BEARER

Mt 11:28-30 ▍ Come unto me, all ye that labor and are heavy laden, and I will give you rest. Take my yoke upon you, and learn of me; for I am meek and lowly in heart: and ye shall find rest unto your soul. For my yoke is easy, and my burden is light.

Isa 53:4-5 ▍ Surely he hath borne our griefs, and carried our sorrows: yet we did esteem him stricken, smitten of God, and afflicted. But he was wounded for our transgressions; he was bruised for our iniquities: the chastisement of our peace was upon him; and with his stripes we are healed.

Isa 53:12 ▍ He hath poured out his soul unto death: and he was numbered with the transgressors; and he bare the sin of many, and made intercession for the transgressors.

Isa 63:8-9 ▍ He said, Surely they are my people, children that will not lie: so he was their Savior. In all their affliction he was afflicted, and the angel of his presence saved them: in his love and in his pity he redeemed them; and he bare them, and carried them all the days of old.

1 Jn 3:5 ▍ And ye know that he was manifested to take away our sins; and in him is no sin.

1 Jn 3:16 ▍ Hereby perceive we the love of God, because he laid down his life for us: and we ought to lay down our lives for the brethren.

Ps 69:9 ▍ For the zeal of thine house hath eaten me up; and the reproaches of them that reproached thee are fallen upon me.

1 Pet 3:18 ▌ For Christ also hath once suffered for sins, the just for the unjust, that he might bring us to God, being put to death in the flesh, but quickened by the Spirit.

GOD'S PLEASURE

1 Chr 29:17 ▌ I know also, my God, that thou triest the heart, and hast pleasure in uprightness. As for me, in the uprightness of mine heart I have willingly offered all these things: and now have I seen with joy thy people, which are present here, to offer willingly unto thee.

Ps 35:27 ▌ Let them shout for joy, and be glad, that favour my righteous cause: yea, let them say continually, Let the Lord be magnified, which hath pleasure in the prosperity of his servant.

Eph 1:5 ▌ Having predestinated us unto the adoption of children by Jesus Christ to himself, according to the good pleasure of his will.

Eph 1:9 ▌ Having made known unto us the mystery of his will, according to his good pleasure which he hath purposed in himself.

Phil 2:13 ▌ For it is God which worketh in you both to will and to do of his good pleasure.

Rev 4:11 ▌ Thou art worthy, O Lord, to receive glory and honour and power: for thou hast created all things, and for thy pleasure they are and were created.

Luke 12:32 ▌ Fear not, little flock; for it is your Father's good pleasure to give you the kingdom.

Prov 5:8 ▌ The sacrifice of the wicked is an abomination to the Lord: But the prayer of the upright is his delight.

Ps 147:11 ▌ The Lord taketh pleasure in them that fear him, in those that hope in his mercy.

Ps 14.9:4 ▎ For the Lord taketh pleasure in his people: He will beautify the meek with salvation.

Heb 13:15-16 ▎ By him therefore let us offer the sacrifice of praise to God continually, that is, the fruit of our lips giving thanks to his name, But to do good and to communicate forget not: for with such sacrifices God is well pleased.

Jer 9:24 ▎ Let him that glorieth glory in this, that he understandeth and knoweth me, that I am the Lord which exercise lovingkindness, judgment, and righteousness, in the earth: for in these things I delight, saith the Lord.

3 Jn 1:4 ▎ I have no greater joy than to hear that my children walk in truth.

Mic 7:18 ▎ Who is a God like unto Thee, that pardoneth iniquity, and passeth by the transgression of the remnant of his heritage? he retaineth not his anger forever, because he delighteth in mercy.

Col 1:19 ▎ It pleased the Father that in him should all fullness dwell.

AVENGER OF HIS ELECT

Luke 18:7-8 ▌ And SHALL NOT GOD AVENGE HIS OWN ELECT, which cry day and night unto him, though he bear long with them? I tell you that HE WILL AVENGE THEM SPEEDILY. Nevertheless when the Son of man cometh, shall he find faith on the earth?

Deut 32:43 ▌ Rejoice, O ye nations, with his people: for HE WILL AVENGE THE BLOOD OF HIS SERVANTS, and will render vengeance to his adversaries, and will be merciful unto his land, and to his people.

Nah 1:2-3 ▌ THE LORD WILL TAKE VENGEANCE ON HIS ADVERSARIES, and HE RESERVETH WRATH FOR HIS ENEMIES. The Lord is slow to anger, and great in power, and will not at all acquit the wicked: the Lord hath his way in the whirlwind and in the storm, and the clouds are the dust of his feet.

Rom 12:19 ▌ Dearly beloved, avenge not yourselves, but rather give place unto wrath: for it is written, VENGEANCE IS MINE; I WILL REPAY, saith the Lord.

Isa 59:18-19 ▌ According to their deeds, ACCORDINGLY HE WILL REPAY, FURY TO HIS ADVERSARIES, RECOMPENSE TO HIS ENEMIES; to the islands he will repay recompense. So shall they fear the name of the Lord from the west, and his glory from the rising of the sun. When the enemy shall come in like a flood, the Spirit of the Lord shall lift up a standard against him.

Ps 94:1-2 ▌ O Lord God, to whom vengeance belongeth; O GOD, TO WHOM VENGEANCE BELONGETH, show thyself. Lift up thyself, thou judge of the earth: render a reward to the proud.

Ps 94:12.13 ▌ Blessed is the man whom thou chastenest, O Lord, and teachest him out of thy law; THAT THOU MAYEST GIVE HIM REST FROM THE DAYS OF ADVERSITY, until the pit be digged for the wicked.

Ps 94:21-23 ▌ They gather themselves together against the soul of the righteous, and condemn the innocent blood. BUT THE LORD IS MY DEFENCE; and my God is the rock of my refuge. And HE SHALL BRING UPON THEM THEIR OWN INIQUITY, and shall cut them off in their own wickedness; yea, the Lord our God shall cut them off.

2 Thess 1:6 ▌ Seeing it is a righteous thing with God TO RECOMPENSE TRIBULATION TO THEM THAT TROUBLE YOU;

1 Thess 4:6 ▌ That no man go beyond and defraud his brother in any matter: because that THE LORD IS THE AVENGER of all such, as we also have forewarned you and testified.

BUT GOD...

Many times as Christians we face adverse circumstances. Disaster and defeat look like they will overwhelm us. BUT GOD IS FAITHFUL!

He delights in helping us to triumph over all adversity.

1 Cor 15:56-57 ▌ The sting of death is sin; and the strength of sin is the law. BUT THANKS BE TO GOD, WHICH GIVETH US THE VICTORY through our Lord Jesus Christ.

Ps 73:26 ▌ My flesh and my heart faileth: BUT GOD IS THE STRENGTH OF MY HEART, and my portion forever.

1 Cor 10:13 ▌ There hath no temptation taken you but such as is common to man: BUT GOD IS FAITHFUL, who will not suffer you to be tempted above that ye are able; but will with the temptation also make a way to escape, that ye may be able to bear it.

Luke 12:19-20 ▌ And I will say to my soul, Soul, thou hast much goods laid up for many years; take thine ease, eat, drink, and be merry. BUT GOD SAID UNTO HIM, THOU FOOL, THIS NIGHT THY SOUL SHALL BE REQUIRED OF THEE: then whose shall those things be, which thou hast provided?

1 Cor 2:9-10 ▌ But as it is written, Eye hath not seen, nor ear heard, neither have entered into the heart of man, the things which God hath prepared for them that love him. BUT GOD HATH REVEALED THEM UNTO US BY HIS SPIRIT: for the Spirit searcheth all things, yea, the deep things of God.

Ps 75:6-7 ▌ For promotion cometh neither from the east, nor from the west, nor from the south. BUT GOD IS THE JUDGE: he putteth down one, and setteth up another.

2 Cor 1:8.9 ▌ For we would not, brethren, have you ignorant of our trouble which came to us in Asia, that we were pressed out of measure, above strength, insomuch that we despaired even of life: But we had the sentence of death in ourselves, that we should not trust in ourselves, BUT IN GOD WHICH RAISETH THE DEAD.

1 Cor 3:6 ▌ I HAVE PLANTED, Apollos watered; BUT GOD GAVE THE INCREASE.

Mark 2:7 ▌ Why doth this man speak blasphemies? WHO CAN FORGIVE SINS BUT GOD ONLY.

Matt 19:26 ▌ But Jesus beheld them, and said unto them, With men this is impossible; BUT WITH GOD ALL THINGS ARE POSSIBLE.

Rom 9:16 ▌ So then it is not of him that willeth, nor of him that runneth, BUT OF GOD THAT SHEWETH MERCY.

Gen 31:5 ▌ And said unto them, I see your father's countenance, that it is not toward me as before; BUT THE GOD OF MY FATHER HATH BEEN WITH ME.

Gen 31:7 ▌ And your father hath deceived me, and changed my wages ten times; BUT GOD SUFFERED HIM NOT TO HURT ME.

Gen 31:42 ▌ If the God of my father, the God of Abraham and the Fear of Isaac, had not been with me, you would surely have sent me away empty-handed. BUT GOD HAS SEEN MY HARDSHIP and the toil of my hands, and last night he rebuked you. (NIV)

Gen 41:16 ▌ "I cannot do it" Joseph replied to Pharaoh, "BUT GOD WILL GIVE PHARAOH THE ANSWER HE DESIRES."(NIV)

Gen 45:6-7 ▌ For two years now there has been famine in the land, and for the next five years there will not be plowing and reaping. BUT GOD SENT ME AHEAD OF YOU TO PRESERVE FOR YOU A REMNANT on earth and to save your lives by a great deliverance. (NIV)

Gen 48:21 ▌ Then Israel said to Joseph, "I am about to die, BUT GOD WILL BE WITH YOU and take you back to the land of your fathers." (NIV)

Gen 50:20 ▌ But as for you, ye thought evil against me; BUT GOD MEANT IT UNTO GOOD, to bring to pass, as it is this day, to save much people alive.

FATHER TO THE FATHERLESS

God cares about the fatherless. He cares about those whose fathers have died or have left them. If you are raising children without a father, it is my prayer that you will know how very precious your children are to God. They hold an extra special place in his heart. His word confirms the favor the fatherless find in him.

Ps 68:5-6 ▎ A FATHER TO THE FATHERLESS, a defender of widows, is God in his holy dwelling. God sets the lonely in families, he leads forth the prisoners with singing; but the rebellious live in a sun-scorched land. (NIV)

Ps 146:9 ▎ The Lord preserveth the strangers; HE RELIEVETH THE FATHERLESS and widow: but the way of the wicked he turneth upside down.

Deut 10:18 ▎ HE DOTH EXECUTE THE JUDGMENT OF THE FATHERLESS and widow, and loveth the stranger, in giving him food and raiment.

Deut 24:19 ▎ When thou cuttest down thine HARVEST in thy field, and hast forgot a sheaf in the field, thou shalt not go again to fetch it: it SHALL BE FOR THE STRANGER, FOR THE FATHERLESS, AND FOR THE WIDOW: that the Lord thy God may bless thee in all the work of thine hands.

Ps 10:14 ▎ The poor committeth himself unto thee; thou art; thou are THE HELPER OF THE FATHERLESS.

Ps 10:17-18 ▎ Lord, thou hast heard the desire of the humble: thou wilt prepare their heart, thou wilt cause thine ear to hear: TO JUDGE THE FATHERLESS and the oppressed, that the man of the earth may no more oppress.

Hosea 14:3 ▌ IN THEE THE FATHERLESS FINDETH MERCY.

Prov 23:10.11 ▌ Remove not the old landmark; and enter not into the fields of the fatherless: FOR THEIR REDEEMER IS MIGHTY; he shall plead their cause with thee.

James 1:27 ▌ Pure religion and undefiled before God and the Father is this, To VISIT THE FATHERLESS AND WIDOWS IN THEIR AFFLICTION, and to keep himself unspotted from the world.

THE GOODNESS OF GOD

Ps 73:1 ▌ TRULY GOD IS GOOD to Israel, even to such as are of a clean heart.

Rom 11:22 ▌ Behold therefore the goodness and severity of God: on them which fell, severity; but TOWARD THEE, GOODNESS, IF THOU CONTINUE IN HIS GOODNESS: otherwise thou also shalt be cut off.

Joel 2:13 ▌ Rend your heart and not your garments. Return to the Lord your God, for he is gracious and compassionate, slow to anger and abounding in love, and he relents from sending calamity. (NIV)

Titus 3:34 ▌ For we ourselves also were SOMETIMES FOOLISH, DISOBEDIENT, DECEIVED, SERVING DIVERS LUSTS AND PLEASURES, LIVING IN MALICE AND HATING ONE ANOTHER. BUT AFTER THAT THE KINDNESS AND LOVE OF GOD OUR SAVIOUR TOWARD MAN APPEARED.

Ex 33:19 ▌ And the Lord said, "I will cause all my goodness to pass in front of you, and I will proclaim my name, the Lord, in your presence. I will have mercy on whom I will have mercy, and I will have compassion on whom I will have compassion." (NIV)

Ps 27:13 ▌ I had fainted, unless I had believed to see the GOODNESS OF THE LORD in the land of the living.

Ps 31:19 ▌ OH HOW GREAT IS THY GOODNESS, which thou hast laid up for them that fear thee; which thou hast wrought for them that trust in thee before the sons of men!

Ps 86:17 ▌ GIVE ME A SIGN OF YOUR GOODNESS, that my enemies may see it and be put to shame, for you, O Lord, have helped me and comforted me. (NIV)

2 Chr 6:14 ▌ O Lord, God of Israel, there is no God like you in heaven or on earth - you who keep your covenant of love with your servants who continue wholeheartedly in your way. (NIV)

Ps 109:21 ▌ But do thou for me, O GOD the Lord, for thy name's sake: because THY MERCY IS GOOD, deliver thou me.

Ps 116:12 ▌ HOW CAN I REPAY THE LORD FOR ALL HIS GOODNESS TO ME? (NIV)

Rom 2:4 ▌ Or despisest thou THE RICHES OF HIS GOODNESS and forbearance and longsuffering; not knowing that THE GOODNESS OF GOD LEADETH THEE TO REPENTANCE?

Ps 34:8 ▌ O taste and see that THE LORD IS GOOD: blessed is the man that trusteth in him.

Acts 10:38 ▌ How God anointed Jesus of Nazareth with the Holy Ghost and with power: WHO WENT ABOUT DOING GOOD, and healing all that were oppressed of the devil; for God was with him.

James 1:17 ▌ EVERY GOOD GIFT AND EVERY PERFECT GIFT IS FROM ABOVE, and cometh down from the Father of lights, with whom is no variableness, neither shadow of turning.

GOD'S THOUGHTS

Ps 139:17 ▌ HOW PRECIOUS ALSO ARE THY THOUGHTS unto me, O God! how great is the sum of them!

Ps 92:5 ▌ How great are your works, O Lord, HOW PROFOUND YOUR THOUGHTS! (NIV)

Pro 1:23 ▌ If you had responded to my rebuke, I would have poured out my heart to you and MADE MY THOUGHTS KNOWN TO YOU. (NIV)

Ps 40:5 ▌ Many, O Lord my God, are thy wonderful works which thou hast done and THY THOUGHTS WHICH ARE TO US-WARD: they cannot be reckoned up in order unto thee: if I would declare and speak of them, they are more than can be numbered.

Ps 40:17 ▌ But I am poor and needy; YET THE LORD THINKETH UPON ME: thou art my help and my deliverer; make no tarrying, O my God.

Isa 55:8 ▌ FOR MY THOUGHTS ARE NOT YOUR THOUGHTS, neither are your ways my ways, saith the Lord.

Isa 55:9 ▌ FOR AS THE HEAVENS ARE HIGHER THAN THE EARTH, SO ARE MY WAYS HIGHER THAN YOUR WAYS, AND MY THOUGHTS THAN YOUR THOUGHTS.

Amos 4:13 ▌ He who forms the mountains, creates the wind, and REVEALS HIS THOUGHTS TO MAN, he who turns dawn to darkness, and treads the high places of the earth - the Lord God Almighty is his name. (NIV)

Jer 29:11 ▌ FOR I KNOW THE THOUGHTS THAT I THINK TOWARD YOU, saith the Lord, thoughts of peace, and not of evil, to give you an expected end.

Matt 9:4 ▌ AND JESUS KNOWING THEIR THOUGHTS said, Wherefore think ye evil in your hearts?

Matt 12:25 ▌ And JESUS KNEW THEIR THOUGHTS, and said unto them, every kingdom divided against itself is brought to desolation; and every city or house divided against itself shall not stand.

Luke 9:47-48 ▌ Jesus, PERCEIVING THE THOUGHTS OF THEIR HEART, took a child, and set him by him, And said unto them, Whosoever shall receive this child in my name receiveth me: and whosoever shall receive me receiveth him that sent me: for he that is least among you all, the same shall be great.

THE COMFORTER

2 Cor 1:3-5 ▮ Blessed be God, even the Father of our Lord Jesus Christ, the Father of mercies, and the GOD OF ALL COMFORT; WHO COMFORTETH US IN ALL OUR TRIBULATION, that we may he able to comfort them which are in any trouble, by the comfort wherewith we ourselves are comforted of God. For as the sufferings of Christ abound in us, so our consolation also aboundeth by Christ.

Isa 40:1-2 ▮ COMFORT YE, COMFORT YE MY PEOPLE, saith your God. Speak ye comfortably to Jerusalem, and cry unto her, that her warfare is accomplished, that her iniquity is pardoned: for she hath received of the Lord's hand double for all her sins.

Ps 23:4 ▮ Yea, though I walk through the valley of the shadow of death, I will fear no evil: for thou art with me; THY ROD AND THY STAFF THEY COMFORT ME.

Ps 119:50 ▮ THIS IS MY COMFORT IN MY AFFLICTION: FOR THY WORD HATH QUICKENED ME.

Isa 51:3 ▮ FOR THE LORD SHALL COMFORT ZION: he will comfort all her waste places; and he will make her wilderness like Eden, and her desert like the garden of the Lord; joy and gladness shall be found therein, thanksgiving, and the voice of melody.

Isa 66:13 ▮ AS ONE WHOM HIS MOTHER COMFORTETH, SO WILL I COMFORT YOU; and ye shall be comforted in Jerusalem.

Ps 71:20-21 ▍ Though you have made me see troubles, many and bitter, you will restore my life again; from the depths of the earth you will again bring me up. YOU WILL INCREASE MY HONOR AND COMFORT ME ONCE AGAIN. (NIV)

Ps 86:17 ▍ Give me a sign of your goodness, that my enemies may see it and be put to shame, for YOU, O LORD, HAVE HELPED ME AND COMFORTED ME. (NIV)

Ps 119:76 ▍ LET, I PRAY THEE, THY MERCIFUL KINDNESS BE FOR MY COMFORT, according to thy word unto thy servant.

Jn 14:16 ▍ And I will pray the Father, and HE SHALL GIVE YOU ANOTHER COMFORTER, that he may abide with you for ever.

Jn 14:18 ▍ I WILL NOT LEAVE YOU COMFORTLESS: I will come to you.

Isa 12:1 ▍ And in that day thou shalt say, O Lord, I will praise thee: though thou wast angry with me, thine anger is turned away, and THOU COMFORTEDST ME.

Isa 57:18 ▍ I have seen his ways, and will heal him: I will lead him also, And RESTORE COMFORTS UNTO HIM AND TO HIS MOURNERS.

Isa 61:1-2 ▍ The Spirit of the Lord GOD is upon me; because the Lord hath anointed me to preach good tidings unto the meek; he hath sent me to bind up the brokenhearted, to proclaim liberty to the captives, and the opening of the prison to them that are bound; to proclaim the acceptable year of the Lord, and the day of vengeance of our God; TO COMFORT ALL THAT MOURN.

THE RESTORER

Ps 23:3 ❙ HE RESTORETH MY SOUL: he leadeth me in the paths of righteousness for his name's sake.

Isa 58:12 ❙ And they that shall be of thee shall build the old waste places: thou shalt raise up the foundations of many generations; and thou shalt be called, The repairer of the breach, THE RESTORER OF PATHS TO DWELL IN.

Ps 51:12 ❙ RESTORE UNTO ME THE JOY OF THY SALVATION; and uphold me with thy free spirit.

Jer 30:17 ❙ FOR I WILL RESTORE HEALTH UNTO THEE, and I will heal thee of thy wounds, saith the Lord; because they called thee an Outcast, saying, This is Zion, whom no man seeketh after.

Isa 44:26 ❙ Who carries out the words of his servants and fulfills the predictions of his messengers, who says of Jerusalem, "It shall be inhabited," of the towns of Judah, "They shall be built," and OF THEIR RUINS, "I WILL RESTORE THEM." (NIV)

Joel 2:25-26 ❙ AND I WILL RESTORE TO YOU THE YEARS THAT THE LOCUST HATH EATEN, the cankerworm, and the caterpiller, and the palmerworm, my great army which I sent among you. And ye shall eat in plenty, and be satisfied, and praise the name of the Lord your God, that hath dealt wondrously with you: and my people shall never be ashamed.

Ps 80:3 ❙ RESTORE US, O GOD; make your face shine upon us, that we may be saved. (NIV)

Isa 49:8 ▌ This is what the Lord says: "In the time of my favor I will answer you, and in the day of salvation I will help you; I will keep you and will make you to be a covenant for the people, TO RESTORE THE LAND and to reassign its desolate inheritances." (NIV)

Isa 57:18 ▌ I have seen his ways, and will heal him: I will lead him also, and RESTORE COMFORTS UNTO HIM AND TO HIS MOURNERS.

Jer 15:19 ▌ Therefore this is what the Lord says: "If you repent, I WILL RESTORE YOU THAT YOU MAY SERVE ME; if you utter worthy, not worthless, words, you will be my spokesman. Let this people turn to you, but you must not turn to them." (NIV)

THE HELPER

Heb 13:6 ▮ So that we may boldly say, THE LORD IS MY HELPER, I will not fear what man shall do unto me.

Ps 116:6 ▮ The Lord preserveth the simple: I was brought low, and HE HELPED ME.

Ex 4:12 ▮ Now go; I WILL HELP YOU SPEAK and will teach you what to say. (NIV)

2 Chr 14:11 ▮ And Asa cried unto the Lord his God, and said, LORD, IT IS NOTHING WITH THEE TO HELP, WHETHER WITH MANY, OR WITH THEM THAT HAVE NO POWER: help us, O Lord our God; for we rest on thee, and in thy name we go against this multitudes. O Lord, thou art our God; let not man prevail against thee.

Deut 33:29 ▮ Blessed are you, O Israel! Who is like you, a people saved by the Lord? HE IS YOUR SHIELD AND HELPER and your glorious sword. Your enemies will cower before you, and you will trample down their high places. (NIV)

Ps 63:7 ▮ Because THOU HAST BEEN MY HELP, therefore in the shadow of thy wings will I rejoice.

Ps 54:4 ▮ Surely GOD IS MY HELP; the Lord is the one who sustains me. (NIV)

Ps 118:7 ▮ The Lord is with me; HE IS MY HELPER. I will look in triumph on my enemies. (N1V)

2 Chr 32:7-8 ▌ Be strong and courageous, be not afraid nor dismayed for the king of Assyria, nor for all the multitudes that is with him: for there be more with us than with him: With him is an arm of flesh; but WITH US IS THE LORD OUR GOD TO HELP US, and to fight our battles. And the people rested themselves upon the words of Hezekiah king of Judah.

Ps 18:6 ▌ In my distress I called to the Lord; I CRIED TO MY GOD FOR HELP. From his temple he heard my voice; my cry came before him, into his ears. (NIV)

Ps 30:2 ▌ O Lord my God, I CALLED TO YOU FOR HELP AND YOU HEALED ME. (NIV)

Ps 72:12 ▌ HE SHALL DELIVER THE NEEDY WHEN HE CRIETH; THE POOR ALSO, AND HIM THAT HATH NO HELPER.

Ex 2:23-24 ▌ During that long period, the king of Egypt died. The Israelites groaned in their slavery and cried out, and THEIR CRY FOR HELP BECAUSE OF THEIR SLAVERY WENT UP TO GOD. God heard their groaning and he remembered his covenant with Abraham, with Isaac and with Jacob. (NIV)

THE GOD WHO LISTENS

Mal 3:16 ▌ Then they that feared the Lord spake often one to another: and the LORD HEARKENED, AND HEARD it, and a book of remembrance was written before him for them that feared the Lord, and that thought upon his name.

1 Ki 17:22 ▌ The LORD HEARD THE VOICE OF ELIJAH; and the soul of the child came into him again, and he revived.

Gen 21:16-17 ▌ And she went, and sat her down over against him a good way off, as it were a bowshot: for she said, Let me not see the death of the child. And she sat over against him, and lift up her voice, and wept. And GOD HEARD THE VOICE OF THE LAD; and the angel of God called to Hagar out of heaven, and said unto her, What aileth thee, Hagar? fear not; for God hath heard the voice of the lad where he is.

Ps 22:24 ▌ For he hath not despised nor abhorred the affliction of the afflicted; neither hath he hid his face from him; but WHEN HE CRIED UNTO HIM, HE HEARD.

2 Chr 7:12 ▌ And the Lord appeared to Solomon by night, and said unto him, I HAVE HEARD THY PRAYER, and have chosen this place to myself for an house of sacrifice.

2 Chr 7:14 ▌ If my people, which are called by my name, shall humble themselves, and pray, and seek my face, and turn from their wicked ways; THEN WILL I HEAR FROM HEAVEN, and will forgive their sin, and will heal their land.

Isa 49:8 ▌ Thus saith the Lord, IN AN ACCEPTABLE TIME HAVE I HEARD THEE, and in a day of salvation have I helped thee: and I will preserve thee, and give thee for a covenant of the people, to establish the earth, to cause to inherit the desolate heritages.

Ps 34:4 ❙ I sought the Lord, AND HE HEARD ME, and delivered me from all my fears.

Ps 34:6 ❙ This poor man cried, and THE LORD HEARD HIM, and saved him out of all his troubles.

Job 22:27 ❙ Thou shalt make thy prayer unto him, and HE SHALL HEAR THEE, and thou shalt pay thy vows.

Ps 55:17 ❙ Evening, and morning, and at noon, will I pray, and cry aloud: and HE SHALL HEAR MY VOICE.

THE FACE OF THE LORD

Ps 31:16 ▮ MAKE THY FACE TO SHINE UPON THY SERVANT: save me for thy mercies sake.

Ps 34:16 ▮ THE FACE OF THE LORD IS AGAINST THEM THAT DO EVIL, to cut off the remembrance of them from the earth.

Ps 27:8 ▮ When thou saidst, SEEK YE MY FACE; my heart said unto thee, thy face, Lord, will I seek.

Ps 30:7 ▮ Lord, by thy favour thou hast made my mountain to stand strong: THOU DIDST HIDE THY FACE, AND I WAS TROUBLED.

Ps 80:3 ▮ Turn us again, O God, and CAUSE THY FACE TO SHINE; and we shall be saved.

Num 6:25 ▮ THE LORD MAKE HIS FACE SHINE UPON THEE, and be gracious unto thee;

Isa 50:6 ▮ I gave my back to the smiters, and my cheeks to them that plucked off the hair: I HID NOT MY FACE FROM SHAME AND SPITTING.

Ezek 15:7 ▮ AND I WILL SET MY FACE AGAINST THEM; they shall go out from one fire, and another fire shall devour them; and ye shall know that I am the Lord, when I set my face against them.

THE GOD OF PATIENCE AND CONSOLATION

Rom 15:5 ▍ NOW THE GOD OF PATIENCE AND CONSOLATION grant you to be likeminded one toward another according to Christ Jesus.

Matt 18:26-27 ▍ The servant therefore fell down, and worshipped him, saying, Lord, have patience with me, and I will pay thee all. THEN THE LORD OF THAT SERVANT WAS MOVED WITH COMPASSION, and loosed him, and forgave him the debt.

1 Tm 1:16 ▍ But for that very reason I was shown mercy so that in me, the worst of sinners, CHRIST JESUS MIGHT DISPLAY HIS UNLIMITED PATIENCE as an example for those who would believe on him and receive eternal life. (NIV)

2 Thess 2:16-17 ▍ Now our Lord Jesus Christ himself, and God, even our Father, which hath loved us, and HATH GIVEN US EVERLASTING CONSOLATION and good hope through grace, Comfort your hearts, and stablish you in every good word and work.

Heb 6:18 ▍ That by two immutable things, in which it was impossible for God to lie, WE MIGHT HAVE A STRONG CONSOLATION, who have fled for refuge to lay hold upon the hope set before us.

Rev 1:9 ▍ I John, who also am your brother, and companion in tribulation, and in the kingdom and PATIENCE OF JESUS CHRIST, was in the isle that is called Patmos, for the word of God, and for the testimony of Jesus Christ.

2 Pet 3:15 ▌ Bear in mind that OUR LORD'S PATIENCE MEANS SALVATION, just as our dear brother Paul also wrote you with the wisdom that God gave him. (NIV)

Gen 5:22-23 ▌ But the fruit of the Spirit is love, joy, peace, patience, kindness, goodness, faithfulness, gentleness and self-control. Against such things there is no law. (NIV)

THE WORD

Ps 119:147 ▌ I prevented the dawning of the morning, and cried: I HOPED IN THY WORD.

Ps 119:170 ▌ Let my supplication come before thee: DELIVER ME ACCORDING TO THY WORD.

Ps 119:9 ▌ WHEREWITHAL SHALL A YOUNG MAN CLEANSE HIS WAY? BY TAKING HEED THERETO ACCORDING TO THY WORD.

Ps 119:11 ▌ THY WORD HAVE I HID IN MINE HEART, THAT I MIGHT NOT SIN AGAINST THEE.

Ps 119:28 ▌ My soul melteth for heaviness: STRENGTHEN THOU ME ACCORDING UNTO THY WORD.

Ps 119:41 ▌ Let thy mercies come also unto me, O Lord, EVEN THY SALVATION, ACCORDING TO THY WORD.

Ps 119:42 ▌ So shall I have wherewith to answer him that reproacheth me: for I TRUST IN THY WORD.

Ps 119:49 ▌ REMEMBER THE WORD UNTO THY SERVANT, UPON WHICH THOU HAST CAUSED ME TO HOPE.

2 Sa 22:31 ▌ As for God, his way is perfect; THE WORD OF THE LORD IS TRIED: he is a buckler to all them that trust in him.

1 Sa 15:23 ▌ For rebellion is as the sin of witchcraft, and stubbornness is as iniquity and idolatry. BECAUSE THOU HAST REJECTED THE WORD OF THE LORD, he hath also rejected thee from being king.

1 Ki 8:56 ▍ Blessed be the Lord, that hath given rest unto his people Israel, according to all that he promised: THERE HATH NOT FAILED ONE WORD OF ALL HIS GOOD PROMISE, which he promised by the hand of Moses his servant.

Ps 33:4-6 ▍ THE WORD OF THE LORD IS RIGHT AND TRUE; He is faithful in all he does. The Lord loves righteousness and justice; the earth is full of his unfailing love.

Ps 119:74 ▍ They that fear thee will be glad when they see me; because I HAVE HOPED IN THY WORD.

Ps 119:89 ▍ For ever, O Lord, THY WORD IS SETTLED IN HEAVEN.

Ps 119:105 ▍ THY WORD IS A LAMP UNTO MY FEET, and a light unto my path.

Ps 119:130 ▍ THE ENTRANCE OF THY WORDS GIVETH LIGHT; it giveth understanding unto the simple.

Jn 1:1-3 ▍ In the beginning was the Word, and the Word was with God, and THE WORD WAS GOD. The same was in the beginning with God. All things were made by him; and without him was not any thing made that was made.

Jn 1:14 ▍ And THE WORD WAS MADE FLESH AND DWELT AMONG US, (and we beheld his glory, the glory as of the only begotten of the Father,) full of grace and truth.

Ps 119:50 ▍ This is my comfort in my affliction, for THY WORD HATH QUICKENED ME.

Ps 119:50 ▍ My comfort in my suffering is this: your

promise preserves my life. (NIV)

Gen 15:1 ❙   After these things the word of the Lord came unto Abram in a vision, saying, Fear not, Abram: I am thy shield, and thy exceeding great reward.

Deut 8:3 ❙   And he humbled thee, and suffered thee to hunger, and fed thee with manna, which thou knewest not, neither did thy fathers know, that he might make thee know that man doth not live by bread only, but BY EVERY WORD THAT PROCEEDETH OUT OF THE MOUTH OF THE LORD DOTH MAN LIVE.

Ps 119:133 ❙   ORDER MY STEPS IN THY WORD: and let not any iniquity have dominion over me.

GOD KNOWS YOU

Matt 6:8 ▌ Be not ye therefore like unto them: for your FATHER KNOWETH WHAT THINGS YE HAVE NEED OF, before ye ask him.

Ps 139:1 ▌ O LORD, THOU HAST SEARCHED ME, AND KNOWN ME.

Ps 139:2 ▌ THOU KNOWEST MY DOWNSITTING AND MINE UPRISING, thou understandest my thought afar off.

Ps 139:4 ▌ There is not a word in my tongue, but, lo, O Lord, thou knowest it altogether.

Ps 1:6 ▌ FOR THE LORD KNOWETH THE WAY OF THE RIGHTEOUS: but the way of the ungodly shall perish.

Jer 29:11 ▌ FOR I KNOW THE THOUGHTS THAT I THINK TOWARD YOU, SAITH THE LORD, thoughts of peace, and not of evil, to give you an expected end.

THE DELIVERER

Job 5:19-26 ❙ From six calamities he will rescue you; in seven no harm will befall you. IN FAMINE HE WILL RANSOM YOU from death, and in battle from the stroke of the sword, YOU WILL BE PROTECTED FROM THE LASH OF THE TONGUE and NEED NOT FEAR DESTRUCTION WHEN IT COMES. You will laugh at destruction and famine, and NEED NOT FEAR THE BEASTS OF THE EARTH. For you will have a covenant with the stones of the field, and the WILD ANIMALS WILL BE AT PEACE WITH YOU. You will know that your tent (house) is secure; you will take stock of your property and find nothing missing. You will know that your children will be many, and your descendants like the grass of the earth. You will come to the grave in full vigor, like sheaves gathered in season. (NIV)

Ps 55:18 ❙ HE HATH DELIVERED MY SOUL in peace from the battle that was against me: for there were many with me.

Ps 97:10 ❙ Ye that love the Lord, hate evil: he preserveth the souls of his saints; HE DELIVERETH THEM OUT OF THE HAND OF THE WICKED.

2 Cor 1:10 ❙ WHO DELIVERED US FROM SO GREAT A DEATH, AND DOTH DELIVER: IN WHOM WE TRUST THAT HE WILL YET DELIVER US.

2 Tm 4:18 ❙ THE LORD SHALL DELIVER ME FROM EVERY EVIL WORK, and will preserve me unto his heavenly kingdom: to whom be glory for ever and ever. Amen.

Job 36:15 ❙ HE DELIVERETH THE POOR IN HIS AFFLICTION, and openeth their ears in oppression.

Jer 1:8 ▌ Be not afraid of their faces: for I AM WITH THEE TO DELIVER THEE, saith the Lord.

Dan 6:27 ▌ HE DELIVERETH AND RESCUETH, and he worketh signs and wonders in heaven and in earth, who hath delivered Daniel from the power of the lions.

Col. 1:13 ▌ WHO HATH DELIVERED US FROM THE POWER OF DARKNESS, and hath translated us into the kingdom of his dear Son.

PRESERVER OF MEN

Ps 121:8 ▌ THE LORD SHALL PRESERVE THY GOING OUT AND THY COMING IN from this time forth, and even for evermore.

Isa 49:8 ▌ Thus said; the Lord, In an acceptable time have I heard thee, and in a day of salvation have I helped thee: and I WILL PRESERVE THEE, and give thee for a covenant of the people, to establish the earth, to cause to inherit the desolate heritages.

Deut 6:24 ▌ And the Lord commanded us to do all these statutes, to fear the Lord our God, for our good always, THAT HE MIGHT PRESERVE US ALIVE, as it is at this day.

Josh 24:17 ▌ For the Lord our God, he it is that brought us up and our fathers out of the land of Egypt, from the house of bondage, and which did those great signs in our sight, and PRESERVED US IN ALL THE WAY WHEREIN WE WENT, and among all the people through whom we passed.

2 Sam 8:6 ▌ Then David put garrisons in Syria of Damascus: and the Syrians became servants to David, and brought gifts. AND THE LORD PRESERVED DAVID WHITHERSOEVER HE WENT.

Ps 31:23 ▌ O love the Lord, all ye his saints: FOR THE LORD PRESERVETH THE FAITHFUL, and plentifully rewardeth the proud doer.

Ps 37:28 ▌ For the Lord loveth judgment, and forsaketh not his SAINTS; they are PRESERVED FOR EVER: but the seed of the wicked shall be cut off.

Ps 146:9 ▮ THE LORD PRESERVETH THE STRANGERS; he relieveth the fatherless and widow: but the way of the wicked he turneth upside down.

2 Tm 4:18 ▮ And the LORD SHALL DELIVER ME FROM EVERY EVIL WORK, AND WILL PRESERVE ME unto his heavenly kingdom: to whom be glory for ever and ever. Amen.

THE GOD OF TRUTH

Jn 8:32 ▮ AND YE SHALL KNOW THE TRUTH, AND THE TRUTH SHALL MAKE YOU FREE.

Isa 65:16 ▮ He who blesseth himself in the earth shall bless himself in THE GOD OF TRUTH; and he that sweareth in the earth shall swear by THE GOD OF TRUTH; because the former troubles are forgotten, and because they are hid from mine eyes.

Ps 91:4 ▮ He shall cover thee with his feathers, and under his wings shalt thou trust: HIS TRUTH SHALL BE THY SHIELD AND BUCKLER.

Jn 14:6 ▮ Jesus saith unto him, I AM THE WAY, THE TRUTH, AND THE LIFE: no man cometh unto the Father, but by me.

A love of the truth sets people free and delivers them.

2 Thess 2:10 ▮ And with all deceivableness of unrighteousness in them that perish; because they received not THE LOVE OF THE TRUTH, that they might be saved.

1 Jn 5:6 ▮ This is he that came by water and blood, even Jesus Christ; not by water only, but by water and blood. And it is the Spirit that beareth witness, because THE SPIRIT IS TRUTH.

3 Jn 1:4 ▮ I HAVE NO GREATER JOY THAN TO HEAR THAT MY CHILDREN WALK IN TRUTH.

Jn 18:37 ▎ Pilate therefore said unto him, Art thou a king then? Jesus answered, Thou sayest that I am a king. To this end was I born, and for this cause came I into the world, THAT I SHOULD BEAR WITNESS UNTO THE TRUTH: EVERY ONE THAT IS OF THE TRUTH HEARETH MY VOICE.

1 Pet 1:22 ▎ Seeing ye have purified your souls in OBEYING THE TRUTH THROUGH THE SPIRIT unto unfeigned love of the brethren, see that ye love one another with a pure heart fervently.

Pr 3:34 ▎ LET NOT MERCY AND TRUTH FORSAKE THEE: bind them about thy neck; write them upon the table of thine heart: So shalt thou find favour and good understanding in the sight of God and man.

Pr 16:6 ▎ BY MERCY AND TRUTH INIQUITY IS PURGED: and by the fear of the Lord men depart from evil.

THE WAY MAKER

2 Sam 22:31 ▮ AS FOR GOD, HIS WAY IS PERFECT; the word of the Lord is tried: he is a buckler to all them that trust in him.

Jer 21:8 ▮ Unto this people thou shalt say, Thus saith the Lord; Behold, I SET BEFORE YOU THE WAY OF LIFE, and the way of death.

Isa 43:16 ▮ Thus saith the Lord, which MAKETH A WAY IN THE SEA, and a path in the mighty waters.

Isa 43:19 ▮ Behold, I will do a new thing; now it shall spring forth; shall ye not know it? I WILL EVEN MAKE A WAY IN THE WILDERNESS, and rivers in the desert.

Jn 14:6 ▮ Jesus saith unto him, I AM THE WAY, THE TRUTH, AND THE LIFE: no man cometh unto the Father, but by me.

Gen 35:3 ▮ And let us arise, and go up to Bethel; and I will make there an altar unto God, who answered me in the day of my distress, and was WITH ME IN THE WAY WHICH I WENT.

Neh 9:19 ▮ Yet thou in thy manifold mercies forsookest them not in the wilderness: the pillar of the cloud departed not from them by day, TO LEAD THEM IN THE WAY; neither the pillar of fire by night, to shew them light, and the way wherein they should go.

Ps 27:11 ▮ TEACH ME THY WAY, O Lord, and lead me in a plain path, because of mine enemies.

Isa 35:8 ▮ And an highway shall be there, and a way, and it shall be called THE WAY OF HOLINESS; the unclean shall not pass over it; but it shall be for those: the wayfaring men, though fools, shall not err therein.

Matt 7:13-14 ❙ Enter ye in at the strait gate: for wide is the gate, and broad is the way, that leadeth to destruction, and many there be which go in thereat: Because strait is the gate, and NARROW IS THE WAY, WHICH LEADETH UNTO LIFE, and few there be that find it.

Heb 10:19.20 ❙ Having therefore, brethren, boldness to enter into the holiest by the blood of Jesus, BY A NEW AND LIVING WAY, which he hath consecrated for us, through the veil, that is to say, his flesh.

THE HAND OF THE LORD

Isa 66:14 ▌ And when ye see this, your heart shall rejoice, and your bones shall flourish like an herb: and THE HAND OF THE LORD SHALL BE KNOWN TOWARD HIS SERVANTS, and his indignation toward his enemies.

Ex 15:6 ▌ Thy RIGHT HAND, O LORD IS BECOME GLORIOUS IN POWER. Thy right hand, O Lord, hath dashed in pieces the enemy.

Neh 2:18 ▌ Then I told them of THE HAND OF GOD WHICH WAS GOOD UPON ME; as also the king's words that he had spoken unto me. And they said, Let us rise up and build. So they strengthened their hands for this good work.

Ps 37:24 ▌ Though he fall, he shall not be utterly cast down: for the Lord UPHOLDETH HIM WITH HIS HAND.

1 Pet 5:6 ▌ HUMBLE YOURSELVES therefore under THE MIGHTY HAND of God, that He may exalt you in due time.

Deut 5:15 ▌ And remember that thou wast a servant in the land of Egypt, and that the Lord thy GOD BROUGHT THEE OUT thence THROUGH A MIGHTY HAND and by a stretched out arm: therefore the Lord thy God commanded thee to keep the Sabbath day.

Ps 32:4-5 ▌ For day and night THY HAND WAS HEAVY UPON ME: my moisture is turned into the drought of summer. Selah. I acknowledged my sin unto thee, and mine iniquity have I not hid. I said, I will confess my transgressions unto the Lord; and thou forgavest the iniquity of my sin. Selah.

1 Chr 4:10 ▌ And Jabez called on the God of Israel, saying, Oh that thou wouldest bless me indeed, and enlarge my coast, and THAT THINE HAND MIGHT BE WITH ME, and that thou wouldest keep me from evil, that it may not grieve me! And God granted him that which he requested.

Jer 15:17 ▌ I sat not in the assembly of the mockers, nor rejoiced; I SAT ALONE BECAUSE OF THY HAND: for thou hast filled me with indignation.

Ezra 8:31 ▌ Then we departed from the river of Ahava on the twelfth day of the first month, to go unto Jerusalem: and THE HAND OF OUR GOD WAS UPON US, and he delivered us from the hand of the enemy, and of such as lay in wait by the way.

Isa 62:3 ▌ THOU SHALT ALSO BE A CROWN OF GLORY IN THE HAND OF THE LORD, and a royal diadem in the hand of thy God.

1 Sam 12:15 ▌ But IF YOU WILL NOT OBEY the voice of the Lord, but rebel against the commandment of the Lord, THEN SHALL THE HAND OF THE LORD BE AGAINST YOU, as it was against your fathers.

Luke 1:66 ▌ And all they that heard them laid them up in their hearts, saying, What manner of child shall this be! AND THE HAND OF THE LORD WAS WITH HIM.

Ex 7:5 ▌ And the Egyptians shall know that I am the Lord, WHEN I STRETCH FORTH MINE HAND UPON EGYPT, and bring out the children of Israel from among them.

Ps 139:5 ▌ Thou hast beset me behind and before, and LAID THINE HAND UPON ME.

Acts 4:29-30 ▌ Now, Lord, behold their threatenings: and grant unto thy servants, that with all boldness they may speak thy word, BY STRETCHING FORTH THINE HAND TO HEAL; and that signs and wonders may be done by the name of thy holy child Jesus.

Ps 31:15 ▌ MY TIMES ARE IN THY HAND: deliver me from the hand of mine enemies, and from them that persecute me.

Isa 51:16 ▌ And I have put my words in thy mouth, and I HAVE COVERED THEE IN THE SHADOW OF MINE HAND, that I may plant the heavens, and lay the foundations of the earth, and say unto Zion, Thou art my people.

THOU

Ps 23:4 ▌ THOU art with me.

Ps 23:5 ▌ THOU preparest a table before me in the presence of mine enemies.

Ps 86:5 ▌ For THOU, Lord, art good and ready to forgive, and plenteous in mercy unto all them that call upon Thee.

Ps 86:7 ▌ In the day of my trouble, I will call upon Thee, for THOU will answer me.

Ps 86:10 ▌ For THOU art great, and doest wondrous things; THOU art God alone.

Ps 86:15 ▌ THOU hast a mighty arm: strong is thy hand, and high is thy right hand.

Acts 2:28 ▌ THOU hast made known to me the ways of life.

Acts 2:28 ▌ THOU shalt make me full of joy with Thy countenance.

Ps 32:7 ▌ THOU art my hiding place.

Ps 32:7 ▌ THOU shalt compass me about with songs of deliverance.

2 Sam 22:40 ▌ THOU hast girded me with strength to battle.

Ps 30:2 ▌ O Lord my God, I cried unto Thee, and THOU hast healed me.

Ps 10:14 ▌ THOU art the helper of the fatherless.

Jer 17:17 ▌ THOU art my hope in the day of evil.

THE HUSBAND TO THE WIDOW

One of the Hebrew words for the widow is 'alma. It means, in the sense of bereavement; discarded, (as a divorced person) forsaken. Taken from Strong's Concordance #4881.

Several other words for widow are taken from this word. What wonderful news for the widow and divorced person! All of God's promises apply to divorced women, as well as widows. God cares for abandoned women.

He loves them and wants them to know that although others may forsake them, He never will. He will always stay faithful, because He has said,

"I will never leave you or forsake you!"

James 1:27 ▌ Pure religion and undefiled before God and the Father is this, To visit the fatherless and widows in their affliction, and to keep himself unspotted from the world.

Ps 146:9 ▌ The Lord preserveth the strangers; HE RELIEVETH THE FATHERLESS AND WIDOW: but the way of the wicked he turneth upside down.

Pr 15:25 ▌ The Lord will destroy the house of the proud: but HE WILL ESTABLISH THE BORDER OF THE WIDOW.

Ex 22:22-23 ▌ YE SHALL NOT AFFLICT ANY WIDOW, OR FATHERLESS CHILD. IF THOU AFFLICT THEM IN ANY WISE, AND THEY CRY AT ALL UNTO ME, I WILL SURELY HEAR THEIR CRY.

Deut 10:18 ▌ HE DEFENDS THE CAUSE OF THE FATHERLESS AND THE WIDOW, and loves the alien, giving him food and clothing.

Deut 14:29 ▌ And the Levite, (because he hath no part, nor inheritance with thee,) and the stranger, and the fatherless, and the widow, which are within thy gates, shall come, and shall eat and be satisfied; that the Lord thy God may bless thee in all the work of thine hand which thou doest.

God blesses those who bless the widow and the fatherless.

Deut 26:12 ▌ When thou hast made an end of tithing all the tithes of thine increase the third year, which is the year of tithing, and hast given it unto the Levite, the stranger, the fatherless, and the widow, that they may eat within thy gates, and be filled.

Deut 27:19 ▌ Cursed be he that perverteth the judgment of the stranger, fatherless, and widow.

Isa 1:17 ▌ Learn to do well; seek judgment, RELIEVE THE OPPRESSED, JUDGE THE FATHERLESS, PLEAD FOR THE WIDOW.

Job 29:13 ▌ The blessing of him that was ready to perish came upon me: and I CAUSED THE WIDOW'S HEART TO SING FOR JOY.

Jer 49:11 ▌ LEAVE THY FATHERLESS CHILDREN, I WILL PRESERVE THEM ALIVE; AND LET THY WIDOWS TRUST IN ME.

Ps 68:5-6 ▌ A father of the fatherless, and a judge of the widows, is God in his holy habitation. God setteth the solitary in families: he bringeth out those which are bound with chains: but the rebellious dwell in a dry land.

Isa 54:4-6 ▌ Fear not; for thou shalt not be ashamed: neither be thou confounded; for thou shalt not be put to shame: for thou shalt forget the shame of thy youth, and shalt not remember the reproach of thy widowhood any more. For THY MAKER IS THINE HUSBAND; the Lord of hosts is his name; and thy Redeemer the Holy One of Israel; The God of the whole earth shall he be called. For the Lord hath called thee as a woman forsaken and grieved in spirit, and a wife of youth, when thou wast refused, saith thy God.

THE NAME OF THE LORD

Reverencing the name of the Lord brings extraordinary blessing, but those who take his name in vain are considered his enemies. Which category are you in?

Ps 139:20 ▌ Thine enemies take thy name in vain.

Mal 4:2 ▌ BUT UNTO YOU THAT FEAR MY NAME SHALL THE SON OF RIGHTEOUSNESS ARISE WITH HEALING IN HIS WINGS; and ye shall go forth, and grow up as calves of the stall.

Ps 20:1 ▌ The Lord hear thee in the day of trouble; THE NAME OF THE GOD OF JACOB DEFEND THEE.

Ps 113:3 ▌ From the rising of the sun unto the going down of the same THE LORD'S NAME IS TO BE PRAISED.

Pro 18:10 ▌ THE NAME OF THE LORD IS A STRONG TOWER: the righteous runneth into it, and is safe.

Joel 2:26 ▌ Ye shall eat in plenty, and be satisfied, and PRAISE THE NAME OF THE LORD YOUR GOD, that hath dealt wondrously with you: and my people shall never be ashamed.

Ps 91:14 ▌ Because he hath set his love upon me, therefore will 1 deliver him: I WILL SET HIM ON HIGH, BECAUSE HE HATH KNOWN MY NAME.

Mal 3:16 ▌ Then they that feared the Lord spake often one to another: and the Lord hearkened, and heard it, AND A BOOK OF REMEMBRANCE WAS WRITTEN BEFORE HIM FOR THEM THAT FEARED THE LORD, AND

THAT THOUGHT UPON HIS NAME.

Mal 1:11 ❙ For from the rising of the sun even unto the going down of the same my name shall be great among the Gentiles; and in every place incense shall be offered unto my name, and a pure offering: for MY NAME SHALL BE GREAT AMONG THE HEATHEN, saith the Lord of hosts.

Matt 6:9 ❙ After this manner therefore pray ye: Our Father which art in heaven, HALLOWED BE THY NAME.

SS 1:3 ❙ Because of the savour of thy good ointments THY NAME IS AS OINTMENT POURED FORTH, therefore do the virgins love thee.

Acts 3:16 ❙ AND HIS NAME THROUGH FAITH IN HIS NAME HATH MADE THIS MAN STRONG, whom ye see and know: yea, the faith which is by him hath given him this perfect soundness in the presence of you all.

Joel 2:32 ❙ And it shall come to pass, that WHOSOEVER SHALL CALL ON THE NAME OF THE LORD SHALL BE DELIVERED: for in mount Zion and in Jerusalem shall be deliverance, as the Lord hath said, and in the remnant whom the Lord shall call.

Isa 9:6 ❙ For unto us a child is born, unto us a son is given: and the government shall be upon his shoulder: and HIS NAME SHALL BE CALLED WONDERFUL, COUNSELLOR, THE MIGHTY GOD, THE EVERLASTING FATHER, THE PRINCE OF PEACE.

THE GOD OF MERCY

1 Tm 1:16 ▎ But for that very reason I WAS SHOWN MERCY SO THAT IN ME, THE WORST OF SINNERS, CHRIST JESUS MIGHT DISPLAY HIS UNLIMITED PATIENCE as an example for those who would believe on him and receive eternal life. (NIV)

Luke 6:36 ▎ Be ye therefore merciful, as YOUR FATHER ALSO IS MERCIFUL.

Lam 3:22 ▎ It is of the Lord's mercies that we are not consumed, because HIS COMPASSIONS FAIL NOT.

Ps 103:11 ▎ For as the heaven is high above the earth, SO GREAT IS HIS MERCY TOWARD THEM THAT FEAR HIM.

Joel 2:13 ▎ And rend your heart, and not your garments, and turn unto the Lord your God: for HE IS GRACIOUS AND MERCIFUL, slow to anger, and of great kindness, and repenteth him of the evil.

Ex 34:6 ▎ And the Lord passed by before him, and proclaimed, The Lord, the Lord God, MERCIFUL AND GRACIOUS, longsuffering, and abundant in goodness and truth.

Mic 7:18 ▎ Who is a God like unto thee, that pardoneth iniquity, and passeth by. the transgression of the remnant of his heritage? he retaineth not his anger forever, because HE DELIGHTETH IN MERCY.

Jer 3:12 ▎ Go and proclaim these words toward the north, and say, return, thou backsliding Israel, saith the Lord; and

I will not cause mine anger to fall upon you: FOR I AM MERCIFUL.

1 Chr 21:13 ❚ David said to God, "I am in deep distress. Let me fall into the hands of the Lord, FOR HIS MERCY IS VERY GREAT; but do not let me fall into the hands of men." (NIV)

Isa 55:7 ❚ Let the wicked forsake his way, and the unrighteous man his thoughts: and let him return unto the Lord, and HE WILL HAVE MERCY UPON HIM; and to our God, for he will abundantly pardon.

Ps 41:4 ❚ I said, LORD, BE MERCIFUL UNTO ME: heal my soul; for I have sinned against thee.

2 Chr 30:9 ❚ If ye turn again unto the Lord, your brethren and your children shall find compassion before them that lead them captive, so that they shall come again into this land: for the Lord your God is gracious and merciful, and will not turn away his face from you.

REVEALER OF SECRETS

Luke 2:26 ❚ IT WAS REVEALED UNTO HIM BY THE HOLY GHOST, that he should not see death, before he had seen the Lord's Christ.

Dan 2:28 ❚ BUT THERE IS A GOD IN HEAVEN THAT REVEALETH SECRETS, and maketh known to the king Nebuchadnezzar what shall be in the latter days. Thy dream, and the visions of thy head upon thy bed, are these.

Amos 3:7 ❚ Surely the Lord GOD will do nothing, but HE REVEALETH HIS SECRET UNTO HIS SERVANTS THE PROPHETS.

Deut 29:29 ❚ The secret things belong unto the Lord our God: but THOSE THINGS WHICH ARE REVEALED BELONG UNTO US and to our children for ever, that we may do all the words of this law.

Eph 1:9 ❚ HAVING MADE KNOWN UNTO US THE MYSTERY OF HIS WILL, according to his good pleasure which he hath purposed in himself.

1 Sam 3:21 ❚ And the Lord appeared again in Shiloh: FOR THE LORD REVEALED HIMSELF TO SAMUEL in Shiloh by the word of the Lord.

1 Sam 9:15 ❚ Now the Lord had told Samuel in his ear a day before Saul came.

Jer 11:18 ❚ AND THE LORD HATH GIVEN ME KNOWLEDGE OF IT, and I know it: then thou shewest me their doings.

1 Cor 2:9-10 ❚ But as it is written, Eye hath not seen,

nor ear heard, neither have entered into the heart of man, the things which God hath prepared for them that love him. But GOD HATH REVEALED THEM UNTO US BY HIS SPIRIT: for the Spirit searcheth all things, yea, the deep things of God.

Dan 2:19 ▌ Then was the SECRET REVEALED UNTO DANIEL in a night vision: Then Daniel blessed the God of heaven.

Matt 11:25 ▌ At that time Jesus answered and said, I thank thee, O Father, Lord of heaven and earth, because thou hast hid these things from the wise and prudent, and, HAST REVEALED THEM UNTO BABES.

Dan 2:22 ▌ HE REVEALETH THE DEEP AND SECRET THINGS: he knoweth what is in the darkness, and the light dwelleth with him.

Gen 41:25 ▌ And Joseph said unto Pharaoh, The dream of Pharaoh is one: GOD HATH SHEWED PHARAOH WHAT HE IS ABOUT TO DO.

Matt 16:17 ▌ And Jesus answered and said unto him, Blessed art thou, Simon Barjona: for FLESH AND BLOOD HATH NOT REVEALED IT UNTO THEE, BUT MY FATHER which is in heaven.

THE EYES OF THE LORD

2 Chr 16:9 ▌ FOR THE EYES OF THE LORD RUN TO AND FRO THROUGHOUT THE WHOLE EARTH, to shew himself strong in the behalf of them whose heart is perfect toward him. Herein thou hast done foolishly: therefore from henceforth thou shalt have wars.

1 Ki 22:43 ▌ And he walked in all the ways of Asa his father; he turned not aside from it, DOING THAT WHICH WAS RIGHT IN THE EYES OF THE LORD: nevertheless the high places were not taken away; for the people offered and burnt incense yet in the high places.

Gen 6:8 ▌ But Noah found GRACE IN THE EYES OF THE LORD.

Jdg 3:12 ▌ And the children of Israel DID EVIL AGAIN IN THE SIGHT OF THE LORD: and the Lord strengthened Eglon the king of Moab against Israel, because they had done evil in the sight of the Lord.

2 Cor 8:21 ▌ Providing for HONEST THINGS, not only IN THE SIGHT OF THE LORD but also in the sight of men.

1 Pet 3:12 ▌ For THE EYES OF THE LORD ARE OVER THE RIGHTEOUS, and his ears are open unto their prayers: but the face of the Lord is against them that do evil.

Pro 22:12 ▌ THE EYES OF THE LORD PRESERVE KNOWLEDGE, and he overthroweth the words of the transgressor.

Pro 5:21 ▍ For the WAYS OF MAN ARE BEFORE THE EYES OF THE LORD and he pondereth all his goings.

Pro15:3 ▍ The EYES OF THE LORD ARE IN EVERY PLACE, beholding the evil and the good.

Pro 33:18 ▍ The EYE OF THE LORD IS UPON THEM THAT FEAR HIM, upon them that hope in his mercy.

OUR INHERITANCE

Acts 26:18 ▌ To open their eyes, and to turn them from darkness to light and from the power of Satan unto God, that THEY MAY RECEIVE FORGIVENESS OF SINS, AND INHERITANCE among them which are sanctified by faith that is in me.

Eph 1:11 ▌ IN WHOM ALSO WE HAVE OBTAINED AN INHERITANCE, being predestinated according to the purpose of him who worketh all things after the counsel of his own will.

Eph 1:14 ▌ Which is THE EARNEST OF OUR INHERITANCE until the redemption of the purchased possession, unto the praise of his glory.

Eph 1:18 ▌ The eyes of your understanding being enlightened; that ye may know what is the hope of his calling, and what the riches of the glory of HIS INHERITANCE IN THE SAINTS.

Rom 8:17 ▌ And if children, then heirs; HEIRS OF GOD, and joint-heirs with Christ; if so be that we suffer with him, that we may be also glorified together.

Isa 49:8 ▌ Thus saith the Lord, In an acceptable time have I heard thee, and in a day of salvation have I helped thee: and I will preserve thee, and give thee for a covenant of the people, to establish the earth, TO CAUSE TO INHERIT THE DESOLATE HERITAGES.

Ps 37:22 ▌ FOR SUCH AS BE BLESSED OF HIM SHALL INHERIT the earth; and they that be cursed of him shall be cut off.

Matt 5:5 ▌ Blessed are the meek: for THEY SHALL INHERIT THE EARTH.

Gal 3:29 ▌ And if ye he Christ's, then are ye Abraham's seed, and HEIRS ACCORDING TO THE PROMISE.

IN THE SHADOW
OF HIS WINGS

Ps 36:7 ▎ How excellent is thy lovingkindness, O God! therefore the children of men put their trust under the SHADOW OF THY WINGS.

Matt 23:37 ▎ O Jerusalem, Jerusalem, thou that killest the prophets, and stoneth them which are sent unto thee, how often would I have gathered thy children together, even as a hen gathereth her chickens under her wings, and ye would not!

Ex 19:4 ▎ Ye have seen what I did unto the Egyptians, and how I BARE YOU ON EAGLES' WINGS, and brought you unto myself.

Ps 17:8-9 ▎ Keep me as the apple of the eye, HIDE ME UNDER THE SHADOW OF THY WINGS, From the wicked that oppress me, from my deadly enemies, who compass me about.

Ruth 2:12 ▎ The Lord recompense thy work, and a full reward be given thee of the Lord God of Israel, UNDER WHOSE WINGS THOU ART COME TO TRUST.

Ps 57:1 ▎ Be merciful unto me, O God, be merciful unto me: for my soul trusted, in thee: yea, IN THE SHADOW OF THY WINGS WILL I MAKE MY REFUGE, until these calamities be overpast.

Ps 91:4 ▎ He shall cover thee with his feathers, and UNDER HIS WINGS SHALT THOU TRUST: his truth shall be thy shield and buckler.

Deut 32:11-12 ▍ As an eagle stirreth up her nest, fluttereth over her young, spreadeth abroad her wings, taketh them, beareth them on her wings: So the Lord alone did lead him, and there was no strange god with him.

Ps 61:4 ▍ I will abide in thy tabernacle for ever: I WILL TRUST IN THE COVERT OF THY WINGS. Selah.

Ps 63:7 ▍ Because thou hast been my help, therefore IN THE SHADOW OF THY WINGS WILL I REJOICE.

Mal 4:2 ▍ But unto you that fear my name shall the Sun of righteousness arise with HEALING IN HIS WINGS; and ye shall go forth, and grow up as calves of the stall.

HEALER OF THE BROKENHEARTED

Ps 147:3 ❙ HE HEALETH THE BROKEN IN HEART, and bindeth up their wounds.

Ps 34:18 ❙ THE LORD IS NIGH UNTO THEM THAT ARE OF A BROKEN HEART; and saveth such as be of a contrite spirit.

Ps 51:17 ❙ The sacrifices of God are a broken spirit: a broken and a contrite heart, O God, thou wilt not despise.

Isa 61:1 ❙ The Spirit of the Lord God is upon me; because the Lord hath anointed me to preach good tidings unto the meek; he hath sent me TO BIND UP THE BROKENHEARTED, to proclaim liberty to the captives, and the opening of the prison to them that are bound.

Eze 34:16 ❙ I will seek that which was lost, and bring again that which was driven away, and will BIND UP THAT WHICH WAS BROKEN, and will strengthen that which was sick: but I will destroy the fat and the strong; I will feed them with judgment.

Luke 4:18 ❙ The Spirit of the Lord is upon me, because he hath anointed me to preach the gospel to the poor; he hath sent me to HEAL THE BROKENHEARTED, to preach deliverance to the captives, and recovering of sight to the blind, to set at liberty them that are bruised.

1 Cor 11:24 ❙ And when he had given thanks, he brake it, and said, Take, eat: THIS IS MY BODY, WHICH IS BROKEN FOR YOU: this do in remembrance of me.

THE GOD OF FAVOR

Pro 11:27 ▌ He that diligently seeketh good procureth favor (NIV).

Pro 3:3-4 ▌ Let not mercy and truth forsake thee: bind them about thy neck; write them upon the table of thine heart: SO SHALT THOU FIND FAVOUR AND GOOD UNDERSTANDING IN THE SIGHT OF GOD and man.

Job 10:12 ▌ THOU HAST GRANTED ME LIFE AND FAVOUR, and thy visitation hath preserved my spirit.

Ex 3:21 ▌ AND I WILL GIVE THIS PEOPLE FAVOUR IN THE SIGHT OF THE EGYPTIANS: and it shall come to pass, that when ye go, ye shall not go empty.

Pro 13:15 ▌ GOOD UNDERSTANDING GIVETH FAVOUR: but the way of transgressors is hard.

Gen 39:21 ▌ But THE LORD was with Joseph, and shewed him mercy, and GAVE HIM FAVOUR IN THE SIGHT OF THE KEEPER OF THE PRISON.

Ps 5:12 ▌ For thou, Lord, WILT BLESS THE RIGHTEOUS; WITH FAVOUR wilt thou compass him as with a shield.

Acts 2:46 47 ▌ And they, continuing daily with one accord in the temple, and breaking bread from house to house, did eat their meat with gladness and singleness of heart, Praising God, and HAVING FAVOUR WITH ALL THE PEOPLE. And the Lord added to the church daily such as should be saved.

Ps 30:5 ▌ For his anger endureth but a moment; IN HIS FAVOUR IS LIFE: weeping may endure for a night, but joy cometh in the morning.

Job 33:26 ▍ He shall pray unto God, and HE WILL BE FAVOURABLE UNTO HIM: and be shall see his face with joy: for He will render unto man his righteousness.

Pro 8:33-35 ▍ HEAR INSTRUCTION, and be wise, and refuse it not. Blessed is the man that heareth me, watching daily at my gates, waiting at the posts of my doors. For whoso findeth me findeth life, and shall OBTAIN FAVOUR OF THE LORD.

WHAT GOD DESIRES

Deut 10:12-13 ▮ And now, Israel, what doth the Lord thy God require of thee, but to FEAR THE LORD thy God, WALK IN ALL HIS WAYS and to LOVE HIM, and to SERVE THE LORD thy God WITH ALL THY HEART AND SOUL, To keep the commandments of the Lord, and his statutes, which I command thee this day for thy good?

Eccl 12:13 ▮ Let us hear the conclusion of the whole matter: FEAR GOD, and KEEP HIS COMMANDMENTS: for this is the whole duty of man.

Hosea 6:6 ▮ For I DESIRED MERCY, and not sacrifice; and the knowledge of God more than burnt offerings.

Mic 6:8 ▮ He hath shewed thee, O man, what is good; and what doth the Lord require of thee, but to DO JUSTLY, and to LOVE MERCY, and to WALK HUMBLY WITH THY GOD?

Rom 13:8 ▮ Owe no man any thing, but to love one another: for HE THAT LOVETH ANOTHER HATH FULFILLED THE LAW.

James 1:27 ▮ Pure religion and undefiled before God and the Father is this, To VISIT THE FATHERLESS AND WIDOWS IN THEIR AFFLICTION, and to keep himself unspotted from the world.

Zech 7:9 ▮ This is what the Lord Almighty says: ADMINISTER TRUE JUSTICE; SHOW MERCY AND COMPASSION to one another. (NIV)

Mark 12:28-31 ▮ And one of the scribes came, and

having heard them reasoning together, and perceiving that he had answered them well, asked him, Which is the first commandment of all? And Jesus answered him, The first of all the commandments is Hear, O Israel; The Lord our God is one Lord: And thou shalt LOVE THE LORD YOUR GOD WITH ALL THY HEART, AND WITH ALL THY SOUL, AND WITH ALL THY MIND AND WITH ALL THY STRENGTH: this is the first commandment. And the second is like, namely this, THOU SHALT LOVE THY NEIGHBOR AS THYSELF. There is none other commandment greater than these.

Mark 12:33 ▌ To LOVE HIM WITH ALL YOUR HEART AND WITH ALL YOUR UNDERSTANDING, and with all the strength, and to love his neighbour as himself, is more than all whole burnt offerings and sacrifices.

Mal 3:8 ▌ Will a man rob God? Yet ye have robbed me. But ye say, Wherein have we robbed thee? In tithes and offerings.

Mal 3:10 ▌ BRING ALL THE TITHES INTO THE STOREHOUSE, that there may be meat in mine house, and prove me now herewith, saith the Lord of hosts, if I will not open you the windows of heaven, and pour you out a blessing, that there shall not be room enough to receive it.

HEALER OF THE SOUL

Ps 142:7 ▌ BRING MY SOUL OUT OF PRISON, that I may praise thy name: the righteous shall compass me about; for thou shalt deal bountifully with me.

Ps 16:10 ▌ FOR THOU WILT NOT LEAVE MY SOUL IN HELL; neither wilt thou suffer thine Holy One to see corruption.

Ps 143:11 ▌ Quicken me, O Lord, for thy name's sake: for thy righteousness' sake BRING MY SOUL OUT OF TROUBLE.

Ps 116:7-8 ▌ RETURN UNTO THY REST, O MY SOUL; for the Lord hath dealt bountifully with thee. FOR THOU HAST DELIVERED MY SOUL FROM DEATH, mine eyes from tears, and my feet from falling.

Ps 23:3 ▌ HE RESTORETH MY SOUL: he leadeth me in the paths of righteousness for his name's sake.

Ps 94:17-19 ▌ Unless the Lord had been my help, MY SOUL HAD ALMOST DWELT IN SILENCE. When I said, My foot slippeth; thy mercy, O Lord, held me up. In the multitudes of my thoughts within me thy comforts delight my soul.

Ps 31:7 ▌ I will be glad and rejoice in thy mercy; for thou hast considered my trouble, THOU HAST KNOWN MY SOUL IN ADVERSITIES.

Ps 41:4 ▌ Lord be merciful unto me: HEAL MY SOUL; for I have sinned against thee.

Ps 19:7 ▌ The law of the Lord is perfect CONVERTING THE SOUL.

CONQUEROR OF SIN

Isa 53:12 ▌ Therefore will I divide him a portion with the great, and he shall divide the spoil with the strong; because he hath poured out his soul unto death: and he was numbered with the transgressors; and he bare the sin of many, and made intercession for the transgressors.

Heb 9:26 ▌ For then must he often have suffered since the foundation of the world: but now once in the end of the world hath he appeared to put away sin by the sacrifice of himself.

Jn 1:29 ▌ The next day John seeth Jesus coming unto him, and saith, Behold the Lamb of God, which taketh away the sin of the world.

Rom 6:23 ▌ For the wages of sin is death; but the gift of God is eternal life through Jesus Christ our Lord.

Eph 1:19-22 ▌ And what is the exceeding greatness of his power to us-ward who believe, according to the working of his mighty power, Which he wrought in Christ, when he raised him from the dead, and set him at his own right hand in the heavenly places, Far above all principality, and power, and might, and dominion, and every name that is named, not only in this world, but also in that which is to come: And hath put all things under his feet and gave him to be the head over all things to the church.

Col 2:13-15 ▌ And you, being dead in your sins and. the uncircumcision of your flesh, hath he quickened together with him, having forgiven you all trespasses; Blotting out the handwriting of ordinances that was against us, which was contrary to us, and took it out of the way, nailing it to his cross; And having spoiled principalities and powers, he made a shew of them openly, triumphing over them in it.

Isa 53:10 ▮ Yet it pleased the Lord to bruise him; be hath put him to grief: when thou shalt make his soul an offering for sin, he shall see his seed, he shall prolong his days, and the pleasure of the Lord shall prosper in his hand.

Rev 3:21 ▮ To him that overcometh will I grant to sit with me in my throne, even as I also overcame, and am set down with my Father in his throne.

1 Jn 3:8 ▮ He that committeth sin is of the devil; for the devil sinneth from the beginning. For this purpose the Son of God was manifested, that he might destroy the works of the devil.

2 Cor 5:21 ▮ For he hath made him to be sin for us, who knew no sin; that we might be made the righteousness of God in him.

Rev 6:2 ▮ And I saw, and behold a white horse: and he that sat on him had a bow; and a crown was given unto him: and he went forth conquering, and to conquer.

BONDAGE BREAKER

Ps 68:6 ▎ God setteth the solitary in families: HE BRINGETH OUT THOSE WHICH ARE BOUND WITH CHAINS: but the rebellious dwell in a dry land.

Ps 116:16 ▎ O Lord, truly I am thy servant; I am thy servant, and the son of thine handmaid: THOU HAST LOOSED MY BONDS.

Gal 5:1 ▎ Stand fast therefore in the liberty wherewith CHRIST HATH MADE US FREE, and be not entangled again with the yoke of bondage.

Isa 9:4 ▎ FOR THOU HAST BROKEN THE YOKE OF HIS BURDEN, and the staff of his shoulder, the rod of his oppressor, as in the day of Midian.

Isa 10:27 ▎ And it shall come to pass in that day, that his burden shall be taken away from off thy shoulder, and his yoke from off thy neck, and THE YOKE SHALL BE DESTROYED BECAUSE OF THE ANOINTING.

Ps 107:20 ▎ He sent his word, and healed them, and DELIVERED THEM FROM THEIR DESTRUCTIONS.

HIS NAME IS JEALOUS

Ex 34:14 ▌ For thou shalt worship no other god: for the Lord, WHOSE NAME IS JEALOUS, is a jealous God:

Deut 4:24 ▌ For the Lord thy God is a consuming fire, EVEN A JEALOUS GOD.

Nah 1:2-3 ▌ GOD IS JEALOUS, and the Lord revengeth; the Lord revengeth, and is furious; the Lord will take vengeance on his adversaries, and he reserveth wrath for his enemies. The Lord is slow to anger, and great in power, and will not at all acquit the wicked: the Lord hath his way in the whirlwind and in the storm, and the clouds are the dust of his feet.

Ezek 39:25 ▌ Therefore thus saith the Lord GOD; Now will I bring again the captivity of Jacob, and have mercy upon the whole house of Israel, and WILL BE JEALOUS FOR MY HOLY NAME.

Deut 5:9-10 ▌ Thou shalt not bow down thyself unto them, nor serve them: for I the Lord thy God AM A JEALOUS GOD, visiting the iniquity of the fathers upon the children unto the third and fourth generation of them that hate me, And shewing mercy unto thousands of them that love me and keep my commandments.

Josh 24:19-20 ▌ HE IS A JEALOUS GOD; he will not forgive your transgressions nor your sins. If ye forsake the Lord, and serve strange gods, then he will turn and do you hurt, and consume you, after that he hath done you good.

Deut 6:15-16 ▌ For the Lord your God, WHO IS AMONG YOU, IS A JEALOUS GOD and his anger will burn against you, and he will destroy you from the face of the land. Do not test the Lord your God as you did at Massah. (NIV)

THE LIFTER OF MY HEAD

James 4:10 ▎ Humble yourselves in the sight of the Lord, and HE SHALL LIFT YOU UP.

Ps 31:1 ▎ In thee, O Lord, do I put my trust; let me never be ashamed: deliver me in thy righteousness.

Ps 3:3 ▎ But thou, O Lord, art a shield for me; my glory, and THE LIFTER UP OF MINE HEAD.

Job 22:29 ▎ When men are cast down, then thou shalt say, THERE IS LIFTING UP; and he shall save the humble person.

Ps 145:14 ▎ THE LORD UPHOLDETH ALL THAT FALL, and raiseth up all those that be bowed down.

Ps 91:11-12 ▎ For he shall give his angels charge over thee, to keep thee in all thy ways. They shall bear thee up in their hands, lest thou dash thy foot against a stone.

1 Sam 2:8 ▎ He raiseth up the poor out of the dust, and LIFTETH UP THE BEGGAR FROM THE DUNGHILL, to set them among princes, and to make them inherit the throne of glory: for the pillars of the earth are the Lord's, and he hath set the world upon them.

1 Pet 5:6 ▎ Humble yourselves, therefore under God's mighty hand, that he may lift you up in due time. (NIV)

THE GOD OF HOPE

1 Pet 3:15 ▌ But in your hearts set apart Christ as Lord. Always be prepared to give an answer to everyone who asks you to GIVE THE REASON FOR THE HOPE THAT YOU HAVE. But do this with gentleness and respect. (NIV)

Ps 33:18 ▌ Behold, the eye of the Lord is upon them that fear him, UPON THEM that HOPE IN HIS MERCY.

Heb 6:18-19 ▌ That by two immutable things, in which it was impossible for God to lie, we might have a strong consolation, who have fled for refuge to LAY HOLD UPON THE HOPE SET BEFORE US: WHICH HOPE WE HAVE AS AN ANCHOR OF THE SOUL, both sure and stedfast, and which entereth into that within the veil.

Ps 39:7 ▌ Now, Lord, what wait I for? MY HOPE IS IN THEE.

Joel 3:16 ▌ The Lord also shall roar out of Zion, and utter his voice from Jerusalem; and the heavens and the earth shall shake: but THE LORD WILL BE THE HOPE OF HIS PEOPLE, and the strength of the children of Israel.

Rom 15:13 ▌ THE GOD OF HOPE fill you with all joy and peace in believing, that ye may abound in hope, through the power of the Holy Ghost.

Jer 17:17 ▌ THOU ART MY HOPE IN THE DAY OF EVIL.

Ps 31:24 ▌ Be of good courage, and he shall strengthen your heart, all YE THAT HOPE IN THE LORD.

Job 11:16.18 ▌ You will surely forget your trouble,

recalling it only as waters gone by. Life will be brighter than noonday, and darkness will become like morning. YOU WILL BE SECURE, BECAUSE THERE IS HOPE; you will look about you and take your rest in safety. (NIV)

Rom 4:18 ❚ WHO AGAINST HOPE BELIEVED IN HOPE, that he might become the father of many nations; according to that which was spoken, So shall thy seed be.

Ps 42:11 ❚ Why art thou cast down, O my soul? and why art thou disquieted within me? HOPE THOU IN GOD; for I shall yet praise him, who is the health of my countenance, and my God.

Hosea 2:15 ❚ There I will give her back her vineyards, and will make the Valley of Achor, (Achor means trouble) a door of hope. There she will sing as in the days of her youth, as in the day she came up out of Egypt. (NIV)

GOD KNOWS YOU

Nah 1:7 ▎ The Lord is good, a strong hold in the day of trouble; and HE KNOWETH THEM THAT I TRUST IN HIM.

Jer 1:5 ▎ BEFORE I FORMED THEE IN THE BELLY I KNEW THEE; and before thou camest forth out of the womb I sanctified thee, and I ordained thee a prophet unto the nations.

2 Tim 2:19 ▎ Nevertheless the foundation of God standeth sure, having this seal, THE LORD KNOWETH THEM THAT ARE HIS. And, Let every one that nameth the name of Christ depart from iniquity.

Ps 94:11 ▎ THE LORD KNOWETH THE THOUGHTS OF MAN, that they are vanity.

2 Cor 11:31 ▎ THE GOD AND FATHER OF OUR LORD JESUS CHRIST, which is blessed for evermore, KNOWETH THAT I LIE NOT.

2 Pet 2:9 ▎ THE LORD KNOWETH HOW TO DELIVER THE GODLY out of temptations, and to reserve the unjust unto the day of judgment to be punished.

THE GOD WHO FORGIVES

Ps 86:5 ▌ For thou, LORD, ART GOOD, AND READY TO FORGIVE; and plenteous in mercy unto all them that call upon thee.

Heb 8:12 ▌ FOR I WILL BE MERCIFUL TO THEIR UNRIGHTEOUSNESS, AND THEIR SINS AND THEIR INIQUITIES WILL I REMEMBER NO MORE.

Isa 43:25 ▌ I, even I, AM HE THAT BLOTTETH OUT THY TRANSGRESSIONS for mine own sake, and will not remember thy sins.

Jer 33:8 ▌ I will cleanse them from all the sin they have committed against me and WILL FORGIVE ALL THEIR SINS OF REBELLION AGAINST ME. (NIV)

Ps 32:5 ▌ Then I acknowledged my sin to you and did not cover up my iniquity. I said, "I will confess my transgressions to the Lord" - and you FORGAVE THE GUILT OF MY SIN. SELAH (NIV)

Matt 26:28 ▌ THIS IS MY BLOOD OF THE COVENANT, WHICH IS POURED OUT FOR MANY FOR THE FORGIVENESS OF SINS. (NIV)

Acts 10:43 ▌ To him give all the prophets witness, that through his name WHOSOEVER BELIEVETH IN HIM SHALL RECEIVE REMISSION OF SINS.

Ps 103:10-12 ▌ He does not treat us as our sins deserve or repay us according to our iniquities. For as high as the heavens are above the earth, so great is his love for those who fear him; as far as the east is from the west, SO FAR HAS HE

REMOVED OUR TRANGRESSIONS FROM US. (NIV)

1 Jn 1:9 ▌ If we confess our sins, HE IS FAITHFUL AND JUST TO FORGIVE US OUR SINS, and to cleanse us from all unrighteousness.

Isa 44:22 ▌ I HAVE BLOTTED OUT, AS A THICK CLOUD, THY TRANSGRESSIONS, and, as a cloud, thy sins: return unto me; for I have redeemed thee.

GOD'S GENTLENESS

Ps 18:35 ❚   Thou hast also given me the shield of thy salvation: and thy right hand hath holden me up, and THY GENTLENESS HATH MADE ME GREAT.

Isa 40:11 ❚   He shall feed his flock like a shepherd: he shall gather the lambs with his arm, and carry them in his bosom, and SHALL GENTLY LEAD THOSE THAT ARE WITH YOUNG.

2 Cor 10:1 ❚   Now I Paul myself beseech you BY THE MEEKNESS AND GENTLENESS OF CHRIST, who in presence am base among you, but being absent am bold toward you.

James 3:17 ❚   But the wisdom that is from above is first pure, then peaceable, gentle, and easy to be intreated, full of mercy and good fruits, without partiality, and without hypocrisy.

GOD ANSWERS PRAYER

Jer 29:11-13 ▮ For I know the thoughts that I think toward you, saith the Lord, thoughts of peace, and not of evil, to give you an expected end. Then ye shall call upon me, and ye shall go and PRAY UNTO ME, AND I WILL HEARKEN UNTO YOU. And ye shall seek me, and find me, when ye shall search for me with all your heart.

Isa 65:24 ▮ And it shall come to pass, that BEFORE THEY CALL, I WILL ANSWER; and while they are yet speaking, I will hear.

James 5:16 ▮ Confess your faults one to another, and pray one for another, that ye may be healed. THE EFFECTUAL FERVENT PRAYER OF A RIGHTEOUS MAN AVAILETH MUCH.

Ps 91:14-15 ▮ Because he hath set his love upon me, therefore will I deliver him: I will set him on high, because he hath known my name. HE SHALL CALL UPON ME, AND I WILL ANSWER HIM: I will be with him in trouble; I will deliver him, and honour him.

Job 33:3 ▮ CALL UNTO ME, AND I WILL ANSWER THEE, and show thee great and mighty things, which thou knowest not.

Ps 66:18-20 ▮ If I regard iniquity in my heart, the Lord will not hear me: But verily God hath heard me; HE HATH ATTENDED TO THE VOICE OF MY PRAYER. Blessed be God, which hath not turned away my prayer, nor his mercy from me.

Jn 22:27 ▌ THOU SHALT MAKE THY PRAYER UNTO HIM, AND HE SHALL HEAR THEE, and thou shalt pay thy vows.

Mark 11:24-25 ▌ Therefore I say unto you, What things soever ye desire, when ye pray, believe that ye receive them, and ye shall have them. And when ye stand praying, forgive, if ye have aught against any: that your Father also which is in heaven may forgive you your trespasses.

Isa 58:9 ▌ THEN SHALT THOU CALL, AND THE LORD SHALL ANSWER; thou shalt cry, and he shall say, Here I am. If thou take away from the midst of thee the yoke, the putting forth of the finger, and speaking vanity.

THE ARM OF THE LORD

Deut 33:27 ▌ The eternal God is thy refuge, and UNDERNEATH ARE THE EVERLASTING ARMS: and he shall thrust out the enemy from before thee; and shall say, Destroy them.

Deut 7:19 ▌ The great temptations which thine eyes saw, and the signs, and the wonders, and the mighty hand, and THE STRETCHED OUT ARM, WHEREBY THE LORD THY GOD BROUGHT THEE OUT: so shall the Lord thy God do unto all the people of whom thou art afraid.

Isa 53:1 ▌ Who hath believed our report? and TO WHOM IS THE ARM OF THE LORD REVEALED?

Ex 6:6 ▌ Wherefore say unto the children of Israel, I am the Lord, and I will bring you out from under the burdens of the Egyptians, and I will rid you out of their bondage, and I WILL REDEEM YOU WITH A STRETCHED OUT ARM, and with great judgments.

Ps 89:13 ▌ THOU HAST A MIGHTY ARM: strong is thy hand, and high is thy right hand.

Ps 98:1 ▌ O sing unto the Lord a new song; for he hath done marvelous things: his right hand, and HIS HOLY ARM, HATH GOTTEN HIM THE VICTORY.

Isa 62:8 ▌ The Lord hath sworn by his right hand, and BY THE ARM OF HIS STRENGTH, Surely I will no more give thy corn to be meat for thine enemies; and the sons of the stranger shall not drink thy wine, for the which thou hast laboured.

Deut 5:15 ▎ And remember that thou wast a servant in the land of Egypt, and that THE LORD THY GOD BROUGHT THEE OUT THENCE THROUGH A MIGHTY HAND AND BY A STRETCHED OUT ARM: therefore the Lord thy God commanded thee to keep the Sabbath day.

STRENGTH IN THE TIME OF TROUBLE

Ps 8:2 ▍ Out of the mouth of babes and sucklings hast THOU ORDAINED STRENGTH BECAUSE OF THINE ENEMIES, that thou mightest still the enemy and the avenger.

Heb 11:33-34 ▍ Who through faith subdued kingdoms, wrought righteousness, obtained promises, stopped the mouths of lions. Quenched the violence of fire, escaped the edge of the sword, OUT OF WEAKNESS WERE MADE STRONG, waxed valiant in fight, turned to flight the armies of the aliens.

2 Sam 22:33 ▍ GOD IS MY STRENGTH AND POWER: and he maketh my way perfect.

Ps 73:26 ▍ My flesh and my heart faileth: but GOD IS THE STRENGTH OF MY HEART, and my portion for ever.

Prov 11:8 ▍ The righteous is delivered out of trouble, and the wicked cometh in his stead.

Ps 46:1 ▍ God is our refuge and strength, a very PRESENT HELP IN TROUBLE.

Ps 28:7 ▍ The LORD IS MY STRENGTH and my shield; my heart trusted in him, and I am helped: therefore my heart greatly rejoiceth; and with my song will I praise him.

Ps 37:39 ▍ But the salvation of the righteous is of the Lord: HE IS THEIR STRENGTH IN THE TIME OF TROUBLE.

Isa 40:28-31 ▍ Hast thou not Known? hast thou not heard, that the everlasting God, the Lord, the Creator of the ends of the earth, fainteth not, neither is weary? there is no searching of his understanding. HE GIVETH POWER TO THE FAINT; AND TO THEM THAT HAVE NO MIGHT HE INCREASETH STRENGTH. Even the youths shall faint and be weary, and the young men shall utterly fall: But THEY THAT WAIT UPON THE LORD SHALL RENEW THEIR STRENGTH; they shall mount up with wings as eagles; they shall run, and not be weary; and they shall walk, and not faint.

Isa 41:10 ▌ Fear thou not; for I am with thee: be not dismayed; for I am thy God: I WILL STRENGTHEN THEE; yea, I will help thee; yea, I will uphold thee with the right hand of my righteousness.

Ps 91:15 ▌ He shall call upon me, and I will answer him: I WILL BE WITH HIM IN TROUBLE; I will deliver him, and honour him.

Dan 11:32 ▌ And such as do wickedly against the covenant shall he corrupt by flatteries: but THE PEOPLE THAT DO KNOW THEIR GOD SHALL BE STRONG, and do exploits.

Ps 31:24 ▌ Be of good courage, and HE SHALL STRENGTHEN YOUR HEART, all ye that hope in the Lord.

GOD'S IFS

1 Jn 1:7 ▌ BUT IF WE WALK IN THE LIGHT, as he is in the light, we have fellowship one with another, and the blood of Jesus Christ his Son cleanseth us from all sin.

1 Jn 1:8 ▌ IF WE SAY THAT WE HAVE NO SIN, we deceive ourselves, and the truth is not in us.

1 Jn 1:10 ▌ IF WE SAY THAT WE HAVE NOT SINNED, we make him a liar, and his word is not in us.

Isa 1:19-20 ▌ IF YE BE WILLING AND OBEDIENT, ye shall eat the good of the land: But if ye refuse and rebel, ye shall be devoured with the sword: for the mouth of the Lord hath spoken it.

Ex 15:26 ▌ And said, IF THOU WILT DILIGENTLY HEARKEN TO THE VOICE OF THE LORD THY GOD, and wilt do that which is right in his sight, and wilt give ear to his commandments, and keep all his statutes, I will put none of these diseases upon thee, which I have brought upon the Egyptians: for I am the Lord that healeth thee.

Jn 8:24 ▌ I said therefore unto you, that ye shall die in your sins: for IF YE BELIEVE NOT THAT I AM HE, ye shall die in your sins.

Jn 15:10 ▌ IF YE KEEP MY COMMANDMENTS, ye shall abide in my love; even as I have kept my Father's commandments, and abide in his love.

Deut 28:1 ▌ And it shall come to pass, IF THOU SHALT HEARKEN DILIGENTLY UNTO THE VOICE OF THE LORD THY GOD, to observe and to do all his commandments which I command thee this day, that the Lord thy God will set thee on high above all nations of the earth.

Deut 28:2 ▌ And all these blessings shall come on thee, and overtake thee, IF THOU SHALT HEARKEN UNTO THE VOICE OF THE LORD THY GOD.

Jn 15:6 ▌ IF A MAN ABIDE NOT IN ME, he is cast forth as a branch, and is withered; and men gather them, and cast them into the fire, and they are burned.

Jn 15:7 ▌ IF YE ABIDE IN ME, and my words abide in you, ye shall ask what ye will, and it shall be done unto you.

2 Chr 7:14 ▌ IF MY PEOPLE, which are called by my name, SHALL HUMBLE THEMSELVES, AND PRAY, AND SEEK MY FACE, AND TURN FROM THEIR WICKED WAYS; then will I hear from heaven, and will forgive their sin, and will heal their land.

Mark 9:23 ▌ Jesus said unto him, IF THOU CANST BELIEVE, all things are possible to him that believeth.

1 Jn 1:6 ▌ IF WE SAY THAT WE HAVE FELLOWSHIP WITH HIM, and walk in darkness, we lie, and do not the truth.

GOD'S FAITHFULNESS

Ps 33:4 ▌ For the word of the Lord is right and true; HE IS FAITHFUL IN ALL HE DOES. (NIV)

Deut 7:9 ▌ Know therefore that the Lord thy God, he is God, the FAITHFUL GOD, which keepeth covenant and mercy with them that love him and keep his commandments to a thousand generations.

Deut 32:4 ▌ He is the Rock, his works are perfect, and all his ways are just. A FAITHFUL GOD WHO DOES NO WRONG, upright and just is he. (NIV)

Zech 8:8 ▌ I will bring them back to live in Jerusalem; they will be my people, and I WILL BE FAITHFUL AND RIGHTEOUS TO THEM as their God. (NIV)

Ps 89:24 ▌ But MY FAITHFULNESS AND MY MERCY SHALL BE WITH HIM: and in my name shall his horn be exalted.

2 Sam 22:26 ▌ TO THE FAITHFUL YOU SHOW YOURSELF FAITHFUL, to the blameless you show yourself blameless. (NIV)

Ps 36:5 ▌ Thy mercy, O Lord, is in the heavens; and THY FAITHFULNESS REACHETH UNTO THE CLOUDS.

Ps 25:10 ▌ ALL THE WAYS OF THE LORD ARE LOVING AND FAITHFUL for those who keep the demands of his covenant. (NIV)

1 Cor 10:13 ▌ There hath no temptation taken you but such as is common to man: but GOD IS FAITHFUL, who will not suffer you to be tempted above that ye are able; but will with the temptation also make a way to escape, that ye may be able to bear it.

Ps 145:13 ▌ Your kingdom is an everlasting kingdom, and your dominion endures through all generations. THE LORD IS FAITHFUL TO ALL HIS PROMISES and loving toward all he has made. (NIV)

Ps 111:7 ▌ THE WORKS OF HIS HANDS ARE FAITHFUL and just; all his precepts are trustworthy. (NIV)

Isa 49:7 ▌ Thus saith the Lord, the Redeemer of Israel, and his Holy One, to whom man despiseth, to him whom the nation abhorreth, to a servant of rulers, Kings shall see and arise, princes also shall worship, because of THE LORD THAT IS FAITHFUL, and the Holy One of Israel, and he shall choose thee.

A FRIEND THAT LOVES AT ALL TIMES

Pro17:17 ❙ A FRIEND LOVETH AT ALL TIMES, and a brother is born for adversity.

Jer 15:13 ❙ Greater love hath no man than this that a man lay down his life for his friends.

Heb 13:5 ❙ Let your conversation be without covetousness; and be content with such things as ye have: for he hath said, I will never leave thee, nor forsake thee.

Pro 22:11 ❙ He who loves a pure heart and whose speech is gracious will have the KING FOR HIS FRIEND. (NIV)

Eccl 4:9-10 ❙ Two are better than one, because they have a good return for their work: If one falls down, HIS FRIEND CAN HELP HIM UP. But pity the man who falls and has no one to help him up! (NIV)

Pro 18:24 ❙ A man that hath friends must shew himself friendly: and THERE IS A FRIEND THAT STICKETH CLOSER THAN A BROTHER.

Jn 15:15 ❙ I no longer call you servants, because a servant does not know his master's business. Instead, I HAVE CALLED YOU FRIENDS, for everything that I learned from my Father I have made known to you. (NIV)

Pro 27:10 ❙ Thine own friend, and thy father's friend, forsake not; neither go into thy brother's house in the day of thy calamity: for better is a neighbour that is near than a brother far off.

SS 5:16 ▮ His mouth is most sweet: yea, he is altogether lovely. THIS IS MY BELOVED, AND THIS IS MY FRIEND, O daughters of Jerusalem.

Luke 5:20 ▮ When Jesus saw their faith, he said, "FRIEND, YOUR SINS ARE FORGIVEN." (NIV)

Matt 11:19 ▮ The Son of man came eating and drinking, and they say, Behold a man gluttonous, and a winebibber, A FRIEND OF PUBLICANS AND SINNERS. But wisdom is justified of her children.

Even though Jesus knew that Judas had come to betray him and turn him over to a horrible death, he remained "The Friend That Loves at all times"

Matt 26:49-50 ▮ Going at once to Jesus, Judas said, "Greetings Rabbi!" and kissed him. Jesus replied, "FRIEND, DO WHAT YOU CAME FOR." (NIV)

FAITHFUL AND TRUE

Rev 19:11 ▎ And I saw heaven opened, and behold a white horse; and he that sat upon him was called FAITHFUL AND TRUE, and in righteousness he doth judge and make war.

1 Thess 5:24 ▎ FAITHFUL IS HE that calleth you, who also will do it.

2 Thess 3:3 ▎ But THE LORD IS FAITHFUL, who shall stablish you, and keep you from evil.

2 Tim 2:13 ▎ If we believe not, yet HE ABIDETH FAITHFUL: he cannot deny himself.

Heb 2:17 ▎ Wherefore in all things it behoved him to be made like unto his brethren, that he might be a merciful and FAITHFUL HIGH PRIEST in things pertaining to God, to make reconciliation for the sins of the people.

Heb 3:1.2 ▎ Wherefore, holy brethren, partakers of the heavenly calling, consider the Apostle and High Priest of our profession, Christ Jesus; WHO WAS FAITHFUL to him that appointed him, as also Moses was faithful in all his house.

Heb 10:23 ▎ Let us hold fast the profession of our faith without wavering; for he is FAITHFUL THAT PROMISED.

1 Jn 1:9 ▎ If we confess our sins, HE IS FAITHFUL AND JUST TO FORGIVE us our sins, and to cleanse us from all unrighteousness.

Rev 1:5 ▎ And from JESUS CHRIST, who is the FAITHFUL WITNESS, and the first begotten of the dead, and the prince of the kings of the earth. Unto him that loved us, and washed us from our sins in his own blood.

THE LIGHT

Jn 8:12 ▌ Then spake Jesus again unto them, saying, I AM THE LIGHT OF THE WORLD: he that followeth me shall not walk in darkness, but shall have the LIGHT OF LIFE.

Ps 27:1 ▌ The LORD IS MY LIGHT and my salvation; whom shall I fear? the Lord is the strength of my life; of whom shall I be afraid?

Jn 1:9 ▌ That was THE TRUE LIGHT, WHICH LIGHTETH EVERY MAN that cometh into the world.

Jn 1:4-5 ▌ In him was life; and THE LIFE WAS THE LIGHT OF MEN. And the LIGHT SHINETH IN DARKNESS; and the darkness comprehended it not.

2 Sam 22:29 ▌ Thou art my lamp, O Lord: and THE LORD WILL LIGHTEN MY DARKNESS.

Isa 9:2 ▌ THE PEOPLE THAT WALKED IN DARKNESS HAVE SEEN A GREAT LIGHT: they that dwell in the land of the shadow of death, UPON THEM HATH THE LIGHT SHINED.

1 Jn 1:5 ▌ This then is the message which we have heard of him, and declare unto you, that GOD IS LIGHT, AND IN HIM IS NO DARKNESS AT ALL.

Mic 7:8 ▌ Rejoice not against me, O mine enemy: when I fall, I shall arise; when I sit in darkness, THE LORD SHALL BE A LIGHT UNTO ME.

Eph 5:14 ▌ Wherefore he saith, Awake thou that sleepest, and arise from the dead, and CHRIST SHALL GIVE THEE LIGHT.

Ps 119:105 ▌ Thy word is a lamp unto my feet, and A LIGHT UNTO MY PATH.

Ps 119:130 ▌ THE ENTRANCE OF THY WORDS GIVETH LIGHT; it giveth understanding unto the simple.

2 Cor 4:6 ▌ FOR GOD, WHO COMMANDED THE LIGHT TO SHINE OUT OF DARKNESS, hath shined in our hearts, to give the light of the knowledge of the glory of God in the face of Jesus Christ.

Isa 60:20 ▌ Thy sun shall no more go down; neither shall thy moon withdraw itself: for THE LORD SHALL BE THINE EVERLASTING LIGHT, and the days of thy mourning shall be ended.

THE PROMISE KEEPER

Gen 18:17-19 ▎ Then the Lord said, Shall I hide from Abraham what I am about to do? Abraham will surely become a great and powerful nation, and all nations on earth will be blessed through him. For I have chosen him, so that he will direct his children and his household after him to keep the way of the Lord by doing what is right and just, so that the LORD WILL BRING about for Abraham WHAT HE HAS PROMISED.

Gen 21:1 ▎ And the LORD VISITED SARAH AS HE HAD SAID, and the LORD DID UNTO SARAH AS HE HAD SPOKEN. For Sarah conceived, and BARE ABRAHAM A SON in his old age, at the set time of WHICH GOD HAD SPOKEN to him.

1 Ki 8:24 ▎ You have kept your PROMISE to your servant David my father; with your mouth you have PROMISED and with your hand YOU HAVE FULFILLED it - as it is today. (NIV)

1 Ki 8:56 ▎ Blessed be the Lord, that hath given rest unto His people Israel, according to all that He promised; there hath not failed one word of all His GOOD PROMISE, which HE PROMISED by the hand of Moses His servant.

Acts 1:4-5 ▎ And, being assembled together with them, commanded them that they should not depart from Jerusalem, but wait for the PROMISE OF THE FATHER, which saith he, ye have heard of me. For John truly baptized with water, but ye shall be baptized with the Holy Ghost not many days hence.

Acts 7:38-39 ▎ Then Peter said unto them, Repent, and

be baptized every one of you in the name of Jesus Christ for the remission of sins, and ye shall receive the gift of the Holy Ghost. For THE PROMISE is UNTO YOU, and TO YOUR CHILDREN, and TO ALL that are AFAR OFF, even as many as the Lord our God shall call.

1 Jn 2:25 ▌ And this is the PROMISE THAT HE HATH PROMISED us, even eternal life.

THE SERVANT

Matt 20:25-28 ▎ Jesus called them together and said, "You know that the rulers of the Gentiles lord it over them, and their high officials exercise authority over them. Not so with you. Instead, whoever wants to become great among you must be your servant, and whoever wants to be first must be your slave - just as the Son of Man did not come to be served, but to serve, and to give his life as a ransom for many." (NIV)

Jn 13:13-16 ▎ Ye call me Master and Lord: and ye say well; for so I am. If I then, your Lord and Master, have washed your feet; ye also ought to wash one another's feet. For I have given you an example, that ye should do as I have done to you. Verily, verily, I say unto you, the servant is not greater than his lord; neither he that is sent greater than he that sent him.

Matt 12:18 ▎ Behold my servant, whom I have chosen; my beloved, in whom my soul is well pleased: I will put my spirit upon him, and he shall shew judgment to the Gentiles.

Mark 9:35 ▎ Sitting down, Jesus called the Twelve and said, "If anyone wants to be first, he must be the very last, and the servant of all." (NIV)

Matt 23:10-12 ▎ Neither be ye called masters: for one is your Master, even Christ. But he that is greatest among you shall be your servant. And whosoever shall exalt himself shall be abased; and he that shall humble himself shall be exalted.

Acts 3:13 ▎ The God of Abraham, Isaac and Jacob, the God of our fathers, has glorified his servant Jesus. You handed him over to be killed, and you disowned him before Pilate, though he had decided to let him go. (NIV)

Acts 3:26 ▌ When God raised up his servant, he sent him first to you to bless you by turning each of you from your wicked ways." (NIV)

Phil 2:7 ▌ But made himself of no reputation, and took upon him the form of a servant, and was made in the likeness of men.

THE FOUNTAIN OF LIFE

Ps 36:9 ▌ FOR WITH THEE IS THE FOUNTAIN OF LIFE: in thy light shall we see light.

Prov 14:27 ▌ THE FEAR OF THE LORD IS A FOUNTAIN OF LIFE, to depart from the snares of death.

Jer 2:13 ▌ For my people have committed two evils; they have forsaken me the FOUNTAIN OF LIVING WATERS, and hewed them out cisterns, broken cisterns, that can hold no water.

Prov 16:22 ▌ UNDERSTANDING IS A FOUNTAIN OF LIFE to those who have it, but folly brings punishment to fools. (NIV)

Joel 3:18 ▌ And it shall come to pass in that day, that the mountains shall drop down new wine, and the hills shall flow with milk, and all the rivers of Judah shall flow with waters, and A FOUNTAIN SHALL COME FORTH OF THE HOUSE OF THE LORD, and shall water the valley of Shittim.

Rev 7:17 ▌ For the Lamb which is in the midst of the throne shall feed them, and shall lead them unto LIVING FOUNTAINS OF WATERS: and God shall wipe away all tears from their eyes.

Prov 10:11 ▌ THE MOUTH OF THE RIGHTEOUS IS A FOUNTAIN OF LIFE, but violence overwhelms the mouth of the wicked. (NIV)

Prov 13:14 ▌ THE LAW OF THE WISE IS A FOUNTAIN OF LIFE, to depart from the snares of death.

Zech 13:1 ▌ In that day there shall be a FOUNTAIN

OPENED to the house of David and to the inhabitants of Jerusalem FOR SIN AND FOR UNCLEANNESS.

THE VOICE OF THE LORD

Dan 9:8-10 ▎ O Lord, to us belongeth confusion of face, to our kings, to our princes, and to our fathers, because we have sinned against thee. To the Lord our God belong mercies and forgiveness, though we have rebelled against him; Neither have we OBEYED THE VOICE OF THE LORD our God, to walk in his laws, which he set before us by his servants the prophets.

Dan 9:11 ▎ Yea, all ISRAEL HAVE TRANSGRESSED thy law, even by departing, that THEY MIGHT NOT OBEY THY VOICE; therefore the curse is poured upon us, and the oath that is written in the law of Moses the servant of God, because we have sinned against him.

Deut 28:1-2 ▎ And it shall come to pass, if thou shalt HEARKEN DILIGENTLY UNTO THE VOICE OF THE LORD thy God, to observe and to do all his commandments which I command thee this day, that the Lord thy God will set thee on high above all nations of the earth: and all these BLESSINGS SHALL COME on thee, and overtake thee, If thou shalt HEARKEN UNTO THE VOICE OF THE LORD thy God.

Deut 28:15 ▎ But it shall come to pass, if THOU WILT NOT HEARKEN UNTO THE VOICE OF THE LORD thy God, to observe to do all his commandments and his statutes which I command thee this day; that ALL THESE CURSES SHALL COME upon thee, and overtake thee.

Deut 30:2-3 ▎ And shalt return unto the Lord thy God, and shalt OBEY HIS VOICE according to all that I command thee this day, thou and thy children, with all thine heart, and with all thy soul; That then the Lord thy GOD WILL TURN THY

CAPTIVITY, and have COMPASSION UPON THEE, and will return and gather thee from all the nations, whither the Lord thy God hath scattered thee.

1 Sam 12:15 ▌ But IF YE WILL NOT OBEY THE VOICE OF THE LORD, but rebel against the commandment of the Lord, then shall THE HAND OF THE LORD BE AGAINST YOU, as it was against your fathers.

Gen 3:8 ▌ They HEARD THE VOICE OF THE LORD God walking in the garden in the cool of the day: and Adam and his wife hid themselves from the presence of the Lord God amongst the trees of the garden.

Ex 15:26 ▌ If thou wilt DILIGENTLY HEARKEN TO THE VOICE OF THE LORD thy God, and wilt do that which is right in His sight, and wilt give ear to His commandments, and keep all His statutes, I will put none of these diseases upon thee, which I have brought upon the Egyptians: for I am the Lord that healeth thee.

Ex 23:22 ▌ But if thou shalt indeed OBEY HIS VOICE, and do all that I speak; then I will be an enemy unto thine enemies, and an adversary unto thine adversaries.

Matt 17:5 ▌ While he yet spake, behold, a bright cloud overshadowed them: and BEHOLD A VOICE OUT OF THE CLOUD, which said, This is My beloved Son, in Whom I am well pleased; hear ye Him.

Ki 19:11-12 ▌ He said, Go forth, and stand upon the mount before the Lord. And, behold, the Lord passed by, and a great and strong wind rent the mountains, and brake in pieces the rocks before the Lord; but the Lord was not in the wind: and after the wind an earthquake; but the Lord was not in the earthquake: and after the earthquake a fire; but the Lord was not in the fire: and after the fire a STILL SMALL VOICE.

Jn 18:37 ▮ Pilate therefore said unto him, Art thou a king then? Jesus answered, Thou sayest that I am a king. To this end was I born, and for this cause came I into the world, that I should bear witness unto the truth. EVERY ONE THAT IS OF THE TRUTH HEARETH MY VOICE.

Acts 9:4 ▮ And he fell to the earth, and heard a voice saying unto him, Saul, Saul, why persecutest thou me?

Dan 10:6 ▮ His body also was like the beryl, and his face as the appearance of lightning, and his eyes as lamps of fire, and his arms and his feet like in colour to polished brass, and the VOICE OF HIS WORDS LIKE THE VOICE OF A MULTITUDE.

GOD IS A GIFT GIVER

Rom 6:23 ▌ For the wages of sin is death; but the gift of God is eternal life through Jesus Christ our Lord.

Eph 2:8 ▌ For by grace are ye saved through faith; and that not of yourselves: it is the gift of God.

Jn 3:16 ▌ For God so loved the world, that he gave his only begotten Son, that whosoever believeth in him should not perish; but have everlasting life.

Rom 11:29 ▌ For the gifts and calling of God are without repentance.

Matt 7:11 ▌ If ye then, being evil, know how to give good gifts unto your children, how much more shall your Father which is in heaven give good things to them that ask him?

WHAT THE LORD HATES

Ps 97:10 ▍ Ye that love the Lord hate evil.

If we really want to love the Lord we must embrace what He loves and reject what He hates.

Pro 6:16-19 ▍ These six things doth the Lord hate: yea, seven are an abomination unto him: a proud look, a lying tongue, and hands that shed innocent blood, an heart that deviseth wicked imaginations, feet that be swift in running to mischief, a false witness that speaketh lies, and he that soweth discord among brethren.

Zech 8:17 ▍ And let none of you imagine evil in your hearts against his neighbour; and love no false oath: for all these are things that I hate, saith the Lord.

Pro 28:9 ▍ He that turneth away his ear from hearing the law, even his prayer shall be abomination.

Luke 16:15 ▍ Ye are they which justify yourselves before men; but God knoweth your hearts: for that which is highly esteemed among men is abomination in the sight of God.

Num 11:1 ▍ And when the people complained, it displeased the Lord: and the Lord heard it; and his anger was kindled.

De 18:10-12 ▍ Do not let your people practice fortune-telling, or use sorcery, or interpret omens, or engage in witchcraft, or cast spells, or function as mediums or psychics, or call forth the spirits of the dead. Anyone who does these things is detestable to the Lord.

Ps 11:5 ▍ The Lord trieth the righteous: but the wicked and him that loveth violence his soul hateth.

Prov 11:20 ▌ They that are of a froward heart are abomination to the Lord.

Prov 12:22 ▌ Lying lips are abomination to the Lord.

Prov 21:27 ▌ The sacrifice of the wicked is abomination: how much more, when he bringeth it with a wicked mind?

Mark 10:13-14 ▌ And they brought young children to him, that he should touch them: and his disciples rebuked those that brought them. But when Jesus saw it, he was much displeased.

Deut 7:25 ▌ The graven images of their gods shall ye burn with fire: thou shalt not desire the silver or gold that is on them, nor take it unto thee, lest thou be snared therein: for it is an abomination to the Lord thy God.

Prov 8:13 ▌ The fear of the Lord is to hate evil: pride, and arrogancy, and the evil way, and the froward mouth, do I hate.

Prov 16:5 ▌ Every one that is proud in heart is an abomination to the Lord: though hand join in hand, he shall not he unpunished.

I WILL

Heb 8:12 ▮ I WILL BE MERCIFUL to their unrighteousness, and their sins and their iniquities will I remember no more.

Heb 13:5 ▮ I WILL NEVER LEAVE THEE, nor forsake thee.

Isa 43:19 ▮ I WILL EVEN MAKE A WAY in the wilderness, and rivers in the desert.

Pro 1:23 ▮ I WILL POUR OUT MY SPIRIT unto you, I WILL make known my words unto you.

Jer 31:13b ▮ I WILL TURN their MOURNING INTO JOY and will comfort them, and make them rejoice from their sorrow.

Rev 3:10 ▮ Because thou hast kept the word of my patience, I also WILL KEEP THEE from the hour of temptation.

Jer 15:21 ▮ I WILL DELIEVER THEE out of the hand of the wicked.

Jer 15:21 ▮ I WILL REDEEM THEE out of the hand of the terrible.

Isa 41:10 ▮ I WILL STRENGTHEN THEE.

Isa 41:10 ▮ I WILL HELP THEE.

Ps 32:8 ▮ I WILL INSTRUCT THEE and teach thee the way which thou shalt go.

Ps 32:8 ▮ I WILL GUIDE THEE with mine eye.

Ex 33:14 ❚ I WILL GIVE THEE REST.

Ex 4:11 ❚ I WILL BE THY MOUTH and teach thee what thou shalt say.

Isa 45:2 ❚ I WILL GO BEFORE THEE and make the crooked places straight.

Isa 45:2 ❚ I WILL BREAK in pieces the gates of brass, and cut in sunder the bars of iron.

Isa 45:3 ❚ I WILL GIVE THEE THE TREASURES OF DARKNESS and hidden riches of secret places, that they mayest know that I, the Lord, which call thee by name, am the God of Israel.

Mal 3:11 ❚ I WILL REBUKE THE DEVOURER for your sakes.

Ps 91:14 ❚ I WILL SET him ON HIGH, because he hath known my name.

Ps 91:15 ❚ He shall call upon me and I WILL ANSWER him.

Ps 91:15 ❚ I WILL BE WITH HIM IN TROUBLE.

Ex 23:25 ❚ ...I WILL TAKE SICKNESS AWAY from the midst of thee.

Ex 23:27 ❚ ...I WILL make all thine enemies turn their backs unto thee.

Jer 33:3 ❚ Call unto me, and I WILL ANSWER thee AND SHEW thee GREAT AND MIGHTY THINGS, which thou knowest not.

Jer 32:40 ▎ ...I WILL MAKE AN EVERLASTING COVENANT with them, that I WILL NOT TURN AWAY from them, to do them good; but I WILL PUT MY FEAR IN THEIR HEARTS, that they shall not depart from me.

Rev 21:6 ▎ ...I WILL GIVE unto him that is athirst of the fountain of THE WATER OF LIFE FREELY.

Jn 14:3 ▎ I WILL come again, and RECEIVE YOU unto myself.

Jer 32:37 ▎ I WILL CAUSE THEM TO DWELL SAFELY.

Jer 32:38 ▎ They shall be my people, and I WILL BE THEIR GOD.

Jer 32:39 ▎ I WILL give them one heart, and one way.

1 Ki 3:14 ▎ And if thou wilt walk in my ways to keep my statutes and my commandments, as thy father David did walk, then I WILL LENGTHEN THY DAYS.

Jer 33:8 ▎ I WILL CLEANSE them from all their iniquity, whereby they have sinned against me.

Jer 33:8 ▎ I WILL PARDON all their iniquities.

Hosea 2:19 ▎ ...I WILL BETROTH THEE unto me in righteousness and judgment, and in lovingkindness, and in mercies.

Jer 29:14 ▎ I WILL TURN AWAY YOUR CAPTIVITY.

Matt 11:28 ▎ I WILL GIVE YOU REST.

Jer 30:17 ▎ I WILL RESTORE HEALTH UNTO THEE.

Jer 30:17 ▎ I WILL HEAL THEE OF THY WOUNDS.

Ezek 36:27 ❙ I WILL PUT MY SPIRIT WITHIN YOU, and cause you to walk in my statutes, and ye shall keep my judgments and do them.

Luke 21:15 ❙ I WILL GIVE you a mouth and WISDOM, which all your adversaries shall not be able to gainsay nor resist.

Jn 6:27 ❙ Him that cometh to me I WILL in no wise cast out.

Isa 43:19 ❙ Behold, I WILL DO A NEW THING; now it shall spring forth.

Jer 33:14 ❙ I WILL perform that good thing which I have promised.

Ex 23:22 ❙ Obey His voice, and do all that I speak; then I WILL BE AN ENEMY UNTO THINE ENEMIES, and an adversary unto thine adversaries.

2 Cor 6:16 ❙ I WILL DWELL IN THEM, and walk in them; and I WILL BE THEIR GOD and they shall be my people.

2 Cor 6:17 ❙ Wherefore come out from among them, and be ye separate, saith the Lord, and touch not the unclean thing; and I WILL RECEIVE YOU.

Prov 8:21 ❙ That I may cause those that love me to inherit substance and I WILL FILL THEIR TREASURES.

Isa 49:25 ❙ I WILL CONTEND with him that contendeth with thee.

Isa 49:25 ❙ I WILL SAVE thy children.

Jn 14:15 ❚ If ye shall ask anything in my name, I WILL DO IT.

Jn 14:21 ❚ He that hath my commandments, and keepeth them, he it is that loveth me; and he that loveth me shall be loved of my Father, and I WILL LOVE HIM and manifest myself to him.

Hosea 2:23 ❚ And I WILL sow her unto me in the earth; and I WILL HAVE MERCY upon her that had not obtained mercy; and I will say to them which were not my people, Thou art My people; and they shall say, Thou art my God.

Hosea 14:4 ❚ I WILL HEAL their backsliding, I WILL LOVE them freely: for mine anger is turned away from him.

Hosea 13:14 ❚ I WILL RANSOM them from the power of the grave; I WILL REDEEM them FROM DEATH: O death, I will be thy plagues; O grave, I will be thy destruction: repentance shall be hid from mine eyes.

Matt 12:7 ❚ Know what this meaneth, I WILL HAVE MERCY, and not sacrifice, ye would not have condemned the guiltless.

Gen 12:3 ❚ And I WILL BLESS them that bless thee, and curse him that curseth thee: and in thee shall all families of the earth be blessed.

THE RIVER OF LIFE

Ezek 47:9 ▪ It shall come to pass, that EVERYTHING THAT LIVETH, WHICH MOVETH, WITHERSOEVER THE RIVERS SHALL COME, SHALL LIVE: and there shall he a very great multitude of fish, because these waters shall come thither: for they shall be healed; and every thing shall live whither the river cometh.

Ps 36:8 ▪ They shall be abundantly satisfied with the fatness of thy house; and THOU SHALT MAKE THEM DRINK OF THE RIVER OF THY PLEASURES.

Jn 4:10 ▪ Jesus answered and said unto her, IF THOU KNEWEST THE GIFT OF GOD, and who it is that saith to thee, Give me to drink; thou wouldest have asked of him, and he would have given thee living water.

Jn 4:14 ▪ BUT WHOSOEVER DRINKETH OF THE WATER THAT I SHALL GIVE HIM SHALL NEVER THIRST; but the water that I shall give him shall be in him a WELL OF WATER SPRINGING UP INTO EVERLASTING LIFE.

Ps 46:4-5 ▪ THERE IS A RIVER, THE STREAMS WHEREOF SHALL MAKE GLAD the city of God, the holy place of the tabernacles of the most High. God is in the midst of her, she shall not be moved: God shall help her, and that right early.

Isa 48:18 ▪ O that thou hadst hearkened to my commandments! then had THY PEACE BEEN AS A RIVER, and thy righteousness as the waves of the sea.

Rev 22:1 ▪ And he shewed me a pure RIVER OF WATER

OF LIFE, clear as crystal, proceeding out of the throne of God and of the Lamb.

Rev 22:17 ▌ The Spirit and the bride say, Come. And let him that heareth say, Come. And let him that is athirst come. And WHOSOEVER WILL, LET HIM TAKE OF THE WATER OF LIFE FREELY.

Jer 17:13-14 ▌ O Lord, the hope of Israel, all that forsake thee shall be ashamed, and they that depart from me shall be written in the earth, because they have forsaken the Lord, THE FOUNTAIN OF LIVING WATERS. Heal me, O Lord, and I shall be healed; save me, and I shall be saved: for thou art my praise.

Jn 7:37-38 ▌ In the last day, that great day of the feast, Jesus stood and cried, saying; If any man thirst, let him come unto me, and drink. HE THAT BELIEVETH ON ME, as the scripture hath said, OUT OF HIS BELLY SHALL FLOW RIVERS OF LIVING WATER.

THE PRINCE OF PEACE

Isa 9:6 ❚ For unto us a child is born, unto us a son is given: and the government shall be upon his shoulder: and his name shall be called Wonderful, Counselor, The mighty God, The everlasting Father, THE PRINCE OF PEACE.

Isa 9:7 ❚ OF THE INCREASE OF HIS GOVERNMENT AND PEACE THERE SHALL BE NO END, upon the throne of David, and upon his kingdom, to order it, and to establish it with judgment and with justice from henceforth even forever. The zeal of the Lord of hosts will perform this.

Col 1:20 ❚ And HAVING MADE PEACE THROUGH THE BLOOD OF HIS CROSS, by him to reconcile all things unto himself; by him, I say, whether they be things in earth, or things in heaven.

Isa 32:17 ❚ AND THE WORK OF RIGHTEOUSNESS SHALL BE PEACE; and the effect of righteousness quietness and assurance forever.

Isa 32:18 ❚ AND MY PEOPLE SHALL DWELL IN A PEACEABLE HABITATION, and in sure dwellings, and in quiet resting places.

Eph 2:14 ❚ FOR HE IS OUR PEACE, who hath made both one, and hath broken down the middle wall of partition between us.

Rom 5:1 ❚ Therefore being justified by faith, WE HAVE PEACE WITH GOD THROUGH OUR LORD JESUS CHRIST.

Isa 53:5 ❚ But he was wounded for our transgressions, he

was bruised for our iniquities: THE CHASTISEMENT OF OUR PEACE WAS UPON HIM; and with his stripes ye are healed.

Isa 26:3 ❙ THOU WILT KEEP HIM IN PERFECT PEACE, whose mind is stayed on thee: because he trusteth in thee.

Acts 10:36 ❙ The word which God sent unto the children of Israel, PREACHING PEACE BY JESUS CHRIST: (he is Lord of all:)

2 Thess 3:16 ❙ NOW THE LORD OF PEACE himself give you peace always by all means. The Lord be with you all.

Isa 57:19 ❙ I create the fruit of the lips; PEACE, PEACE TO HIM THAT IS FAR OFF, and to him that is near, saith the Lord; and I will heal him.

Col 3:15 ❙ AND LET THE PEACE OF GOD RULE IN YOUR HEARTS, to the which also ye are called in one body; and be ye thankful.

Jn 14:27 ❙ PEACE I LEAVE WITH YOU, my peace I give unto you: not as the world giveth, give I unto you. Let not your heart be troubled, neither let it be afraid.

THE RESCUER

2 Sam 22:18-20 ▌ He rescued me from my powerful enemy, from my foes, who were too strong for me. They confronted me in the day of my disaster, but the LORD was my support. He brought me out into a spacious place; he rescued me because he delighted in me.

Ps 107:19-20 ▌ Then they cried to the LORD in their trouble, and he saved them from their distress. He sent forth his word and healed them; he rescued them from the grave.

2 Sam 22:48-49 ▌ He is the God who avenges me, who puts the nations under me, who sets me free from my enemies. You exalted me above my foes; from violent men you rescued me.

Neh 9:27 ▌ So you handed them over to their enemies, who made them suffer. But in their time of trouble they cried to you, and you heard them from heaven. In your great mercy, you sent them liberators who rescued them from their enemies.

Ps 18:17 ▌ He rescued me from my powerful enemies, from those who hated me and were too strong for me.

Acts 7: 9-10 ▌ These patriarchs were jealous of their brother Joseph, and they sold him to be a slave in Egypt. But God was with him and rescued him from all his troubles. And God gave him favor before Pharaoh, king of Egypt. God also gave Joseph unusual wisdom, so that Pharaoh appointed him governor over all of Egypt and put him in charge of the palace.

Prov 11:8 ▌ The righteous man is rescued from trouble, and it comes on the wicked instead.

Dan 6:27 ▍ He delivereth and rescueth, and he worketh signs and wonders in heaven and in earth, who hath delivered Daniel from the power of the lions.

Col 1:13 ▍ For he has rescued us from the dominion of darkness and brought us into the kingdom of the Son he loves,

The God of Life

Ps 116:6 ▎ The Lord protects those of childlike faith; I was facing death, and he saved me.

Isa 55:3 ▎ Give ear and come to me; hear me, that your soul may live. I will make an everlasting covenant with you, my faithful love promised to David.

Jer 38:20 ▎ "They will not hand you over," Jeremiah replied. "Obey the Lord by doing what I tell you. Then it will go well with you, and your life will be spared."

Ezek 3:21 ▎ Nevertheless if thou warn the righteous man, that the righteous sin not, and he doth not sin, he shall surely live, because he is warned; also thou hast delivered thy soul.

Ps 119:116 ▎ Uphold me according unto thy word, that I may live: and let me not be ashamed of my hope.

Ps 16:11 ▎ Thou wilt shew me the path of life: in thy presence is fulness of joy; at thy right hand there are pleasures for evermore.

Prov 14:30 ▎ A sound heart is the life of the flesh: but envy the rottenness of the bones.

Ps 54:4 ▎ But God is my helper. The Lord keeps me alive!

Ps 118:13 ▎ My enemies did their best to kill me, but the Lord rescued me.

Ps 118:17 ▎ I shall not die, but live, and declare the works of the Lord.

Section II

The Holy Spirit

THE SPIRIT

Rom 8:1 ❙ There is therefore now no condemnation to them which are in Christ Jesus, who walk not after the flesh, but after THE SPIRIT.

Rom 8:2 ❙ For the law of THE SPIRIT of life in Christ Jesus hath made me free from the law of sin and death.

Rom 8:5 ❙ For they that are after the flesh do mind the things of the flesh; but they that are after THE SPIRIT the things of THE SPIRIT.

Rom 8:9 ❙ But ye are not in the flesh, but in THE SPIRIT, if so be that THE SPIRIT of God dwell in you.

Rom 8:11 ❙ But if THE SPIRIT of him that raised up Jesus from the dead dwell in you, he that raised up Christ from the dead shall also quicken your mortal bodies by his Spirit that dwelleth in you.

Rom 8:14 ❙ For as many as are led by THE SPIRIT of God, they are the sons of God.

Rom 8:23 ❙ Ourselves also, which have the firstfruits of THE SPIRIT.

Rom 8:26 ❙ Likewise THE SPIRIT also helpeth our infirmities: for we know not what we should pray for as we ought: but THE SPIRIT itself maketh intercession for us with groanings which cannot be uttered.

Rom 8:27 ❙ And he that searcheth the hearts knoweth what is the mind of THE SPIRIT, because he maketh intercession for the saints according to the will of God.

Gal 4:6 ▌ And because ye are sons, God hath sent forth THE SPIRIT of his Son into your hearts, crying, Abba, Father.

THE HOLY SPIRIT LIVES IN US

Ezek 36:27 ❙ And I will put my SPIRIT WITHIN YOU, and cause you to walk in my statutes, and ye shall keep my judgments, and do them.

Rom 8:9 ❙ But ye are not in the flesh, but in the Spirit, if so be that the SPIRIT OF GOD DWELL IN YOU. Now if any man have not the Spirit of Christ, he is none of his.

1 Cor 3:16 ❙ Know ye not that ye are the temple of God, and that the SPIRIT OF GOD DWELLETH IN YOU?

1 Jn. 4:12 ❙ No man hath seen God at any time. If we love one another, GOD DWELLETH IN US, and his love is perfected in us.

1 Cor 6:19 ❙ What? know ye not that your body is the temple of the HOLY GHOST which is IN YOU, which ye have of God, and ye are not your own?

1 Jn 3:24 ❙ And he that keepeth his commandments dwelleth in him, and he in him. And hereby we know that he abideth in us, by the Spirit which he hath given us.

DIRECTS

Acts 10:19-20 ▌ While Peter thought on the vision, the Spirit said unto him, Behold, three men seek thee. Arise therefore, and get thee down, and go with them, doubting nothing: for I have sent them.

Acts 13:2 ▌ As they ministered to the Lord, and fasted, the Holy Ghost said, Separate me Barnabas and Saul for the work whereunto I have called them.

Acts 16:6 ▌ Now when they had gone throughout Phrygia and the region of Galatia, and were forbidden of the Holy Ghost to preach the word in Asia.

Rom 8:14 ▌ For as many as are led by the Spirit of God, they are the sons of God.

HE IS THE SPIRIT OF ADOPTION

Rom 8:15.16 ▌ For ye have not received the spirit of bondage again to fear; but ye have received the Spirit of adoption, whereby we cry, Abba, Father. The Spirit itself beareth witness with our spirit, that we are the children of God.

GIVES POWER

Acts 1:8 ▌ But ye shall receive power, after that the Holy Ghost is come upon you: and ye shall be witnesses unto me both in Jerusalem, and in all Judea, and in Samaria, and unto the uttermost part of the earth.

Acts 10:38 ▌ God anointed Jesus of Nazareth with the Holy Ghost and with power: Who went about doing good, and healing all that were oppressed of the devil; for God was with Him.

Acts 4:33 ▌ And with great power gave the apostles witness of the resurrection of the Lord Jesus: and great grace was upon them all.

Luke 4:14 ▌ And Jesus returned in the power of the Spirit into Galilee: and there went out a fame of him through all the region round about.

BRINGS JOY

Rev 14:17 ▍ For the kingdom of God is not meat and drink; but righteousness, and peace, and joy in the Holy Ghost.

Acts 13:52 ▍ The disciples were filled with joy, and with the Holy Ghost.

Rom 15:13 ▍ Now the God of hope fill you with all joy and peace in believing, that ye may abound in hope, through the power of the Holy Ghost.

1 Thess 1:6 ▍ Ye became followers of us, and of the Lord, having received the word in much affliction, with joy of the Holy Ghost.

Gal 5:22 ▍ But the fruit of the Spirit is love, joy, peace, longsuffering, gentleness, goodness, faith.

Acts 8:39 ▍ When they were come up out of the water, the Spirit of the Lord caught away Philip, that the eunuch saw him no more: and he went on his way rejoicing.

HE IS THE SPIRIT OF TRUTH

1 Jn 5:6 ▮ This is he that came by water and blood, even Jesus Christ; not by water only, but by water and blood. And it is the Spirit that beareth witness, because the Spirit is truth. ▮

Jn 15:26 ▮ But when the Comforter is come, whom I will send unto you from the Father, even the Spirit of truth, which proceedeth from the Father, he shall testify of me.

Jn 16:13 ▮ Howbeit when he, the Spirit of truth, is come, he will guide you into all truth: for he shall not speak of himself; but whatsoever he shall hear, that shall he speak: and he will show you things to come.

1 Jn 4:6 ▮ We are of God: he that knoweth God heareth us; he that is not of God heareth not us. Hereby know we the spirit of truth, and the spirit of error.

1 Pet 1:22 ▮ Seeing ye have purified your souls in obeying the truth through the Spirit unto unfeigned love of the brethren, see that ye love one another with a pure heart fervently.

COMFORTS

Jn 14:16-17 ❙ And I will pray the Father, and he shall give you another Comforter, that he may abide with you for ever; even the Spirit of truth; whom the world cannot receive, because it seeth him not, neither knoweth him: but ye know him; for he dwelleth with you, and shall be in you.

Jn 15:26-27 ❙ But when the Comforter is come, whom I will send unto you from the Father, even the Spirit of truth, which proceedeth from the Father, he shall testify of me: and ye also shall bear witness, because ye have been with me from the beginning.

Jn 16:7 ❙ Nevertheless I tell you the truth; It is expedient for you that I go away: for if I go not away, the Comforter will not come unto you; but if I depart, I will send him unto you.

Jn 14:26 ❙ But the Comforter, which is the Holy Ghost, whom the Father will send in my name, he shall teach you all things, and bring all things to your remembrance, whatsoever I have said unto you.

GUIDES

Luke 4:1 ▌ And Jesus being full of the Holy Ghost returned from Jordan, and was led by the Spirit into the wilderness.

Jn 16:13 ▌ Howbeit when he, the Spirit of truth, is come, he will guide you into all truth: for he shall not speak of himself; but whatsoever he shall hear, that shall he speak: and he will show you things to come.

Acts 8:39 ▌ And when they were come up out of the water, the Spirit of the Lord caught away Philip, that the eunuch saw him no more: and he went on his way rejoicing.

2 Pet 1:21 ▌ For the prophecy came not in old time by the will of man: but holy men of God spake as they were moved by the Holy Ghost.

TEACHES

Neh 9:20 ▎ Thou gavest also thy good spirit to instruct them, and withheldest not thy manna from their mouth, and gavest them water for their thirst.

Luke 12:12 ▎ The Holy Ghost shall teach you in the same hour what ye ought to say.

1 Cor 2:13 ▎ Which things also we speak, not in the words which man's wisdom teacheth, but which the Holy Ghost teacheth; comparing spiritual things with spiritual.

1 Jn 2:27 ▎ But the anointing which ye have received of him abideth in you, and ye need not that any man teach you: but as the same anointing teacheth you of all things, and is truth, and is no lie, and even as it hath taught you, ye shall abide in him.

Jn 14:26 ▎ But the Comforter, which is the Holy Ghost, whom the Father will send in my name, he shall teach you all things, and bring all things to your remembrance, whatsoever I have said unto you.

HE BRINGS LIFE

Jn 6:63 ▎ It is the spirit that quickeneth; the flesh profiteth nothing: the words that I speak unto you, they are spirit, and they are life.

Rom 8:10-11 ▎ If Christ be in you, the body is dead because of sin; but the Spirit is life because of righteousness. But if the Spirit of him that raised up Jesus from the dead dwell in you, he that raised up Christ from the dead shall also quicken your mortal bodies by his Spirit that dwelleth in you.

Jn 3:5-6 ▎ Jesus answered, Verily, verily, I say unto thee, Except a man be born of water and of the Spirit, he cannot enter into the kingdom of God. That which is born of the flesh is flesh; and that which is born of the Spirit is spirit.

Rom. 8:2 ▎ For the law of the Spirit of life in Christ Jesus hath made me free from the law of sin and death.

2 Cor 3:6 ▎ Who also hath made us able ministers of the new testament; not of letter, but of the spirit: for the letter killeth, but the spirit giveth life.

1 Pet 3:18 ▎ For Christ also hath once suffered for sins, the just for the unjust, that he might bring us to God, being put to death in the flesh, but quickened by the Spirit.

HE SHOWS THINGS TO COME

Acts 10:19-20 ▌ While Peter thought on the vision, the Spirit said unto him, Behold, three men seek thee. Arise therefore, and get thee down, and go with them, doubting nothing: for I have sent them.

Jn 16:13-14 ▌ When he, the Spirit of truth, is come, he will guide you into all truth: for he shall not speak of himself; but whatsoever he shall hear, that shall he speak: and he will show you things to come. he shall glorify me: for he shall receive of mine, and shall show it unto you.

1 Pet 1:11 ▌ Searching what, or what manner of time the Spirit of Christ which was in them did signify, when it testified beforehand the sufferings of Christ, and the glory that should follow. ▌

1 Cor 2:10 ▌ But God hath revealed them unto us by his Spirit: for the Spirit searcheth all things, yea, the deep things of God.

1 Cor 2:11 ▌ For what man knoweth the things of a man, save the spirit of man which is in him? Even so the things of God knoweth no man, but the Spirit of God.

HELPS OVERCOME WEAKNESSES

Rom 8:26 ▌ Likewise the Spirit also helpeth our infirmities: for we know not what we should pray for as we ought: but the Spirit itself maketh intercession for us with groanings which cannot be uttered.

Gal 5:16 ▌ This I say then, Walk in the Spirit, and ye shall not fulfil the lust of the flesh.

HE BRINGS FREEDOM

Rom 8:1-2   There is therefore now no condemnation to them which are in Christ Jesus, who walk not after the flesh, but after the Spirit. For the law of the Spirit of life in Christ Jesus hath made me free from the law of sin and death.

2 Cor 3:17   Now the Lord is that Spirit: and where the Spirit of the Lord is, there is liberty.

HE CAN BE GRIEVED

Isa 63:10 ▍ They rebelled, and vexed his holy Spirit: therefore he was turned to be their enemy, and he fought against them.

Acts 5:3-4 ▍ But Peter said, Ananias, why hath Satan filled thine heart to lie to the Holy Ghost, and to keep back part of the price of the land? Whiles it remained, was it not thine own? And after it was sold, was it not in thine own power? why hast thou conceived this thing in thine heart? thou hast not lied unto men, but unto God.

Eph 4:30 ▍ And grieve not the holy Spirit of God, whereby ye are sealed unto the day of redemption.

1 Thess 5:19 ▍ Quench not the Spirit.

Heb 10:29 ▍ Of how much sorer punishment, suppose ye, shall he be thought worthy, who hath trodden under foot the Son of God, and hath counted the blood of the covenant, wherewith he was sanctified, an unholy thing, and hath done despite unto the Spirit of grace?

HE BEARS WITNESS

1 Jn 5:8 ▌ There are three that bear witness in earth, the Spirit, and the water, and the blood: and these three agree in one.

1 Jn 5:6 ▌ This is he that came by water and blood, even Jesus Christ; not by water only, but by water and blood. And it is the Spirit that beareth witness, because the Spirit is truth.

Rom 8:16 ▌ The Spirit itself beareth witness with our spirit, that we are the children of God.

GIFTS OF THE HOLY SPIRIT

1 Cor 12:4 ❙ Now there are diversities of gifts, but the same Spirit.

1 Cor 12:7-10 ❙ But the manifestation of the Spirit is given to every man to profit withal. For to one is given by the Spirit the word of wisdom; to another the word of knowledge by the same Spirit; to another faith by the same Spirit; to another the gifts of healing by the same Spirit; to another the working of miracles; to another prophecy; to another discerning of spirits; to another divers kinds of tongues; to another the interpretation of tongues.

Acts 2:38 ❙ Then Peter said unto them, Repent, and be baptized every one of you in the name of Jesus Christ for the remission of sins, and ye shall receive the gift of the Holy Ghost.

Acts 10:45-46 ❙ And they of the circumcision which believed were astonished, as many as came with Peter, because that on the Gentiles also was poured out the gift of the Holy Ghost. For they heard them speak with tongue, and magnify God.

BLASPHEMING THE HOLY SPIRIT

Matt. 12:31 ▌ Wherefore I say unto you, All manner of sin and blasphemy shall be forgiven unto men: but the blasphemy against the Holy Ghost shall not be forgiven unto men.

The devil has used this verse of scripture to condemn and torment many Christians. We cannot take one scripture and make a doctrine out of it. We are told to compare scripture with scripture. Consider these scriptures in light of this.

Jn 6:44 ▌ No man can come to me, except the Father which hath sent me draw him.

Jn 6:37 ▌ Him that cometh to me I will in no wise cast out.

Gal 4:6 ▌ Because ye are sons, God hath sent forth the Spirit of his Son into your hearts, crying, Abba, Father.

1 Jn 4:13 ▌ Hereby know we that we dwell in him, and he in us, because he hath given us of his Spirit.

Isa 11:2 ▌ And the spirit of the Lord shall rest upon him, the spirit of wisdom and understanding, the spirit of counsel and might, the spirit of knowledge and of the fear of the Lord.

Do you still have the fear of the Lord? Do you still cry to God, your Father for help? Do you still desire to be a Christian and go to Heaven? God's Word tells us we cannot come to God, unless He draws us to himself. If you had blasphemed the Holy Spirit, He would have immediately left you. Without God's Spirit drawing you, you would have no desire for God. You would not desire to repent. You would have no fear of the Lord. Your heart would be hardened. The fact that you are even interested in reading this shows you have not blasphemed the Holy Spirit

If you feel a need to be reconciled to God, pray this prayer, call out to God and he will hear you and answer.

Jesus, you said that whosoever comes to you, you'll never cast out. I'm coming to you, Lord. Please forgive me for grieving you, Holy Spirit. I count the blood of Jesus a very precious thing. I esteem you, Lord, and treasure our friendship. Precious Savior, cleanse me from all sins. Help me to live a life that is pleasing to you. Come Holy Spirit and fill me once again. Thank You for your sweet fellowship.

> And the Spirit and the bride say, Come.
> And let him that heareth say, Come.
> And let him that is athirst come.
> And whosoever will, let him take the water of life freely.
> Rev 22:17

Section III

What You Have In Christ

GIFTS OF THE SON

Rom 5:15 ❚ But not as the offence, so also is the free gift. For if through the offence of one many be dead, much more the grace of God, and the gift by grace, which is by one man, Jesus Christ, hath abounded unto many.

Rom 5:17 ❚ For if by one man's offence death reigned by one; much more they which receive abundance of grace and of the gift of righteousness shall reign in life by one, Jesus Christ.

Jn 4:10 ❚ Jesus answered and said unto her, If thou knewest the gift of God, and who it is that saith to thee, 'Give me to drink; thou wouldest have asked of him, and he would have given thee living water.

Eph 4:7-8 ❚ But unto every one of us is given grace according to the measure of the gift of Christ. Wherefore he saith, When he ascended up on high, he led captivity captive, and gave gifts unto men.

I AM

Mark 8:29 ▍ But whom say ye that I AM?

Gen 15:1 ▍ I AM thy SHIELD and thy EXCEEDING GREAT REWARD.

Isa 43:25 ▍ I AM HE THAT BLOTTETH OUT THY TRANSGRESSIONS for mine own sake, and will not remember thy sins.

Matt 28:20 ▍ I AM WITH YOU ALWAYS, even unto the end of the world.

Ps 119:63 ▍ I AM A COMPANION of all them that fear thee and of them that keep thy precepts.

Heb 1:17 ▍ Fear not, I AM the FIRST AND THE LAST.

Jer 32:27 ▍ I AM the Lord, THE GOD OF ALL FLESH: is there any thing too hard for me?

Jn 14:6 ▍ I AM the WAY, the TRUTH, and the LIFE.

Pro 8:14 ▍ I AM UNDERSTANDING.

Ps 35:3 ▍ I AM THY SALVATION.

Jer 9:24 ▍ I AM the Lord which exercise LOVING-KINDNESS, JUDGMENT, and RIGHTEOUSNESS in the earth: for in these things I delight, saith the Lord.

Isa 48:17 ▍ I AM the Lord thy God which TEACHETH thee to profit.

Lev 20:8 ▍ IAM the Lord which SANCTIFY you.

Ex 15:26 ▎ I AM the Lord that HEALETH thee.

Ps 73:23 ▎ I AM CONTINUALLY WITH THEE.

Isa 44:24 ▎ I AM the Lord that maketh all things.

Isa 45:5 ▎ I AM the Lord, and there is none else, there is no God beside me.

Luke 3:14 ▎ I AM that I AM.

Rev 1:18 ▎ I AM HE THAT LIVETH, and was dead; and, behold, I AM ALIVE for evermore. Amen.

Jn 6:35 ▎ I AM the BREAD OF LIFE: he that cometh to me shall never hunger; and he that believeth on me shall never thirst.

Jn 9:5 ▎ I AM the LIGHT OF THE WORLD.

Jn 10:9 ▎ I AM the DOOR.

Jn 10:10 ▎ I AM COME THAT THEY MIGHT HAVE LIFE and that they might have it more abundantly.

Jn 10:11 ▎ I AM the GOOD SHEPHERD: the Good Shepherd giveth his life for the sheep.

Jn 11:25 ▎ I AM the RESURRECTION AND THE LIFE.

Jn 13:13 ▎ Ye call me MASTER and LORD and ye say well; for so I AM.

Jn 15:1 ▎ I AM the TRUE VINE.

Luke 22:27 ▎ I AM among you as HE THAT SERVETH.

Jn 16:32 ▎ I AM NOT ALONE, because the Father is with me.

1 Pet 1:16 ▮ I AM HOLY.

Isa 51:12 ▮ I AM HE THAT COMFORTETH you.

Jer 15:20 ▮ I AM WITH THEE to save thee and to deliver thee.

Jn 6:41 ▮ I AM the BREAD which came down FROM HEAVEN.

Jn 6:51 ▮ I AM the LIVING BREAD.

Rev 22:16 ▮ I AM the ROOT and the OFFSPRING OF DAVID.

Mal 3:6 ▮ I AM the Lord, I change not.

SS 2:1 ▮ I AM the ROSE OF SHARON and the LILY OF THE VALLEY.

Gen 17:1 ▮ I AM THE ALMIGHTY GOD; walk before me and be thou perfect.

Gen 28:15 ▮ I AM WITH THEE and will keep thee in all places wither thou goest.

Ex 22:27 ▮ I AM GRACIOUS.

Matt 11:29 ▮ I AM MEEK AND LOWLY IN HEART.

Ps 46:10 ▮ Be still and know that I AM GOD.

IN THE LORD

Eph 5:8 ▌ For ye were sometimes darkness, but now are ye LIGHT IN THE LORD: walk as children of light.

Eph 6:10 ▌ Finally, my brethren, be STRONG IN THE LORD, and in the power of His might.

Phil 4:4 ▌ REJOICE IN THE LORD always and again I say, Rejoice.

Col 4:17 ▌ Take heed to the ministry which thou halt RECEIVED IN THE LORD, that thou fulfil it.

1 Thess 3:8 ▌ For now we live, if ye STAND FAST IN THE LORD.

1 Thess 5:12 ▌ And we beseech you, brethren, to KNOW THEM which labour among you, and are OVER YOU IN THE LORD, and admonish you.

1 Cor 1:31 ▌ He that glorieth, let him GLORY IN THE LORD.

1 Cor 15:58 ▌ Therefore, my beloved brethren, be ye steadfast, unmovable, always ABOUNDING IN THE WORK OF THE LORD, forasmuch as ye know that your labour is not in vain in the Lord.

Ps 32:11 ▌ BE GLAD IN THE LORD, and rejoice, ye righteous: and shout for joy, all ye that are upright in heart.

Ps 34:2 ▌ MY SOUL SHALL MAKE HER BOAST IN THE LORD: the humble shall hear thereof, and be glad.

Ps 104:34 ▍ My meditation of him shall be sweet: I will BE GLAD IN THE LORD.

Eph 2:21 ▍ In whom all the building fitly framed together GROWETH UNTO AN HOLY TEMPLE IN THE LORD.

IN WHOM

Eph 1:7 ▍ IN WHOM we have REDEMPTION through his blood, the forgiveness of sins, according to the riches of his grace.

Eph 1:11 ▍ IN WHOM also we have obtained AN INHERITANCE.

Eph 1:13 ▍ IN WHOM YE also TRUSTED, after that ye heard the word of truth, the gospel of your salvation: in whom also after that ye believed, ye were sealed with that Holy Spirit of promise.

Eph 2:21 ▍ IN WHOM all the building fitly framed together GROWETH UNTO AN HOLY TEMPLE in the Lord.

Eph 2:22 ▍ IN WHOM ye also are BUILDED TOGETHER for an habitation of God through the Spirit.

Eph 3:12 ▍ IN WHOM we have BOLDNESS and access with confidence by the faith of him.

Col 2:3 ▍ IN WHOM are hid all the TREASURES OF WISDOM and knowledge.

Col 2:11 ▍ IN WHOM also ye are CIRCUMCISED with the circumcision made without hands, in putting off the body of the sins of the flesh by the circumcision of Christ.

1 Pet 1:8 ▍ Whom having not seen, ye love; IN WHOM, though now ye see him not, yet believing, YE REJOICE with joy unspeakable and full of glory.

Rom 10:14 ▌ How then shall they call on him in whom they have not believed? and how shall they BELIEVE IN HIM of whom they have not heard? and how shall they hear without a preacher?

THROUGH HIS BLOOD

Heb 9:11-12 ▌ But Christ being come an high priest of good things to come, by a greater and more perfect tabernacle, not made with hands, that is to say, not of this building; Neither by the blood of goats and calves, but BY HIS OWN BLOOD He entered in once into the holy place, having obtained ETERNAL REDEMPTION for us.

Heb 9:14 ▌ How much more shall THE BLOOD OF CHRIST, who through the eternal Spirit offered himself without spot to God, PURGE YOUR CONSCIENCE from dead works to serve the living God?

Heb 10:19 ▌ Having therefore, brethren, BOLDNESS to enter into the holiest BY THE BLOOD OF JESUS.

1 Jn 1:7 ▌ But if we walk in the light, as he is in the light, we have fellowship one with another, and the BLOOD OF JESUS CHRIST his son CLEANSETH US FROM ALL SIN.

Eph 1:7 ▌ In whom we have REDEMPTION THROUGH HIS BLOOD, the forgiveness of sins.

Rev 5:9 ▌ Thou art worthy to take the book, and to open the seals thereof: for thou wast slain, and hast REDEEMED US TO GOD BY THY BLOOD.

Rom 5:9 ▌ Much more then, being now JUSTIFIED BY HIS BLOOD, we shall be saved from wrath through him.

Rom 3:25 ▌ Whom God hath set forth to be a propitiation through FAITH IN HIS BLOOD, to declare his righteousness for the remission of sins that are past.

Col 1:20 ▌ And, having made PEACE THROUGH THE

BLOOD of his cross, by Him to reconcile all things unto himself.

Rev 12:11 ❙ And they OVERCAME him BY THE BLOOD of the Lamb, and by the word of their testimony.

Heb 12:24 ❙ And to Jesus the mediator of the new covenant, and to THE BLOOD of sprinkling, that SPEAKETH better things than that of Abel.

1 Pet 1:2 ❙ Elect according to the foreknowledge of God the Father, through sanctification of the Spirit, unto obedience and sprinkling of THE BLOOD OF JESUS CHRIST.

Matt 26:28 ❙ For this is MY BLOOD of the new testament, which is shed for many for the REMISSION OF SINS.

Rev 1:5 ❙ And from Jesus Christ, who is the faithful witness, and the first begotten of the dead, and the prince of the kings of the earth. Unto him that loved us, and WASHED US from our sins IN HIS OWN BLOOD.

Heb 13:20 ❙ Now the God of peace, that brought again from the dead our Lord Jesus, that great shepherd of the sheep, THROUGH THE BLOOD of the everlasting covenant, make you perfect in every good work to do his will, working in you that which is well pleasing in his sight, through Jesus Christ; to whom be glory for ever and ever. Amen.

Heb 13:12 ❙ Wherefore Jesus also, that He might SANCTIFY the people WITH HIS OWN BLOOD, suffered without the gate.

Eph 2:13 ❙ But now in Christ Jesus ye who sometimes were far off are MADE NIGH BY THE BLOOD OF CHRIST.

IN THE NAME OF JESUS

Matt 18:20 ▌ For where two or three are gathered together IN MY NAME, there am I in the midst of them.

Mark 16:17-18 ▌ And these signs shall follow them that believe; IN MY NAME shall they CAST OUT DEVILS; they shall speak with NEW TONGUES; They shall TAKE UP SERPENTS; and if they drink any deadly thing, it shall not hurt them; they shall LAY HANDS ON THE SICK, and they shall recover.

Jn 14:13 ▌ And whatsoever ye shall ask IN MY NAME, that will I do, THAT THE FATHER MAY BE GLORIFIED in the Son.

Jn 16:23 ▌ And in that day ye shall ask me nothing. Verily, verily, I say unto you, whatsoever ye shall ASK the Father IN MY NAME, he will give it you.

Jn 16:24 ▌ Hitherto have ye asked nothing IN MY NAME: ask, and YE SHALL RECEIVE, that your joy may be full.

1 Cor 6:11 ▌ Ye are WASHED, but ye are SANCTIFIED, but ye are JUSTIFIED IN THE NAME OF THE LORD JESUS, and by the Spirit of our God.

Col 3:17 ▌ And whatsoever ye DO IN WORD OR DEED, do all IN THE NAME of the Lord Jesus.

Jn 3:18 ▌ He that believeth on him is not condemned: but he that believeth not is condemned already, because he hath not believed IN THE NAME OF THE ONLY BEGOTTEN SON OF GOD.

Joel 2:32 ▌ It shall come to pass, that whosoever shall call

ON THE NAME OF THE LORD shall be DELIVERED: for in mount Zion and in Jerusalem shall be deliverance, as the Lord hath said, and in the remnant whom the Lord shall call.

Jn 5:13 ▌ These things have I written unto you that BELIEVE ON THE NAME OF THE SON OF GOD; that ye may know that ye have eternal life, and that ye may believe on the name.

BY HIM

1 Cor 1:15 ▌ That in every thing ye are ENRICHED BY HIM, in all utterance, and in all knowledge.

Col 1:16 ▌ For BY HIM were ALL THINGS CREATED, that are in heaven, and that are in earth, visible and invisible, whether they be thrones, or dominions, or principalities, or powers: all things were created BY HIM, and for him.

Col 1:17 ▌ And he is before all things, and BY HIM ALL THINGS CONSIST.

Col 1:20 ▌ Having made peace through the blood of his cross, BY HIM to RECONCILE all things unto himself.

Col 3:17 ▌ And whatsoever ye do in word or deed, do all in the name of the Lord Jesus, GIVING THANKS to God and the Father BY HIM.

Heb 7:25 ▌ He is able also to SAVE them to the uttermost that come unto God BY HIM, seeing he ever liveth to make intercession for them.

Heb 13:15 ▌ BY HIM therefore let us offer the SACRIFICE OF PRAISE to God continually, that is, the fruit of our lips giving thanks to his name.

1 Pet 1:21 ▌ Who BY HIM DO BELIEVE IN GOD, that raised him up from the dead, and gave him glory; that your faith and hope might be in God.

WITH CHRIST

Rom 6:8 ▌ Now if we be DEAD WITH CHRIST, we believe that we shall also live with him.

Gal 2:20 ▌ I am CRUCIFIED WITH CHRIST: nevertheless I live; yet not I, but Christ liveth in me: and the life which I now live in the flesh I live by the faith of the Son of God, who loved me, and gave himself for me.

Col 3:1 ▌ If ye then be RISEN WITH CHRIST, seek those things which are above.

Col 3:3 ▌ For ye are dead, and your life is HID WITH CHRIST in God.

Heb 20:4 ▌ They lived and REIGNED WITH CHRIST a thousand years.

THROUGH CHRIST

Rom 5:1 ▌ Therefore being justified by faith, we have peace with God THROUGH our Lord JESUS CHRIST.

Rom 5:11 ▌ And not only so, but we also joy in God THROUGH our Lord JESUS CHRIST, by whom we have now received the atonement.

Rom 6:11 ▌ Reckon ye also yourselves to be dead indeed unto sin, but alive unto God THROUGH JESUS CHRIST our Lord.

Rom 6:23 ▌ The wages of sin is death; but the gift of God is eternal life THROUGH JESUS CHRIST our Lord.

1 Cor 15:57 ▌ Thanks be to God, which giveth us the victory THROUGH our Lord JESUS CHRIST.

Gal 3:13-14 ▌ CHRIST hath redeemed us from the curse of the law, being made a curse for us: for it is written, Cursed is every one that hangeth on a tree: that the blessing of Abraham might come on the Gentiles THROUGH JESUS CHRIST.

Gal 4:7 ▌ Wherefore thou art no more a servant, but a son; and, if a son, then an heir of God THROUGH CHRIST.

Eph 2:7 ▌ That in the ages to come he might show the exceeding riches of his grace in his kindness toward us THROUGH CHRIST JESUS.

Phil 4:6-7 ▌ Be careful for nothing; but in every thing by prayer and supplication with thanksgiving let your requests be made known unto God. And the peace of God, which passeth all understanding, shall keep your hearts and minds THROUGH CHRIST JESUS.

THE FEAR OF THE LORD

The fear of the Lord is to hold God in reverential esteem.

Deut 10:12-13 ▮ Now, Israel, what doth the Lord thy God require of thee, but to FEAR THE LORD THY GOD, to walk in all his ways, and to love him, and to serve the Lord thy God with all thy heart and with all thy soul, to keep the commandments of the Lord, and his statutes, which I command thee this day for thy good?

Ps 89:7 ▮ GOD IS GREATLY TO BE FEARED in the assembly of the saints, and to be had in reverence of all them that are about him.

Pro 1:7 ▮ THE FEAR OF THE LORD is the beginning of knowledge.

Deut 13:4 ▮ Ye shall walk after the Lord your God, and FEAR HIM, and keep his commandments, and obey his voice, and ye shall serve him, and cleave unto him.

Josh 4:24 ▮ That all the people of the earth might know the hand of the LORD, that it is mighty: that ye might FEAR THE LORD your God for ever.

Josh 24:14 ▮ Now therefore FEAR THE LORD, and serve him in sincerity and in truth: and put away the gods which your fathers served on the other side of the flood, and in Egypt; and serve ye the Lord.

2 Chr 19:7 ▮ Let the FEAR OF THE LORD be upon you; take heed and do it.

Pro 3:7 ▍ Be not wise in thine own eyes: FEAR THE LORD, and depart from evil.

Eccl 12:13 ▍ Let us hear the conclusion of the whole matter: FEAR GOD, and keep his commandments: for this is the whole duty of man.

Isa 8:13 ▍ Sanctify the LORD of hosts himself; and LET HIM BE YOUR FEAR, and let him be your dread.

THE COMPASSION OF JESUS

Jesus had compassion on those plagued with insanity.

Mark 5:19 ▌ Howbeit JESUS suffered him not, but saith unto him, Go home to thy friends, and tell them how great things the Lord hath done for thee, and hath HAD COMPASSION on thee.

Jesus had compassion of diseases of every kind.

Matt 9:35-36 ▌ And Jesus went about all the cities and villages, teaching in their synagogues, and preaching the gospel of the kingdom, and healing every sickness and every disease among the people. But when He saw the multitudes, HE WAS MOVED WITH COMPASSION on them, because they fainted, and were scattered abroad, as sheep having no shepherd.

Jesus had compassion of those headed toward destruction and tried to warn them.

Matt 23:37 ▌ O Jerusalem, Jerusalem, thou that killest the prophets, and stonest them which are sent unto thee, how often would I have gathered thy children together, even as a hen gathereth her chickens under her wings, and ye would not!

Jesus had compassion of those with long term and incurable diseases.

Mark 1:41 ▌ And JESUS, MOVED WITH COMPASSION, put forth his hand, and touched him, and saith unto him, I will; be thou clean.

Jesus had compassion on those going through grief and death.

Luke 7:12-13 ▌ When he came nigh to the gate of the city, behold, there was a dead man carried out, the only son of his mother, and she was a widow: and much people of the city was with her. And when the Lord saw her, HE HAD COMPASSION ON HER, and said unto her, Weep not.

Jesus had compassion on all that were sick.

Matt 14:14 ▌ And Jesus went forth, and saw a great multitudes, and was MOVED WITH COMPASSION TOWARD THEM, and he healed their sick.

Jesus had compassion on the blind.

Matt 20:30 ▌ Two blind men sitting by the way side, when they heard that Jesus passed by, cried out, saying, Have mercy on us, O Lord, thou son of David.

Matt 20:32-34 ▌ And Jesus stood still, and called them, and said, what will ye that I shall do unto you? They say unto him, Lord, that our eyes may be opened. So JESUS HAD COMPASSION ON THEM, and touched their eyes: and immediately their eyes received sight, and they followed him

Jesus had compassion of the hungry and weak.

Matt 15:32 ▌ Jesus called his disciples unto him, and said, I HAVE COMPASSION ON THE MULTITUDES, because they continue with me now three days, and have nothing to eat: and I will not send them away fasting, lest they faint in the way.

GODS GUIDANCE

Ps 32:8 ❙ I will instruct thee and teach thee in the way which thou shalt go: I WILL GUIDE THEE WITH MINE EYE.

Ps 48:14 ❙ For this God is our God for ever and ever: HE WILL BE OUR GUIDE EVEN UNTO DEATH.

Isa 30:21 ❙ And THINE EARS SHALL HEAR A WORD BEHIND THEE, saying, THIS IS THE WAY, walk ye in it, when ye turn to the right hand, and when ye turn to the left.

Isa 58:11 ❙ AND THE LORD SHALL GUIDE THEE CONTINUALLY, and satisfy thy soul in drought, and make fat thy bones: and thou shalt be like a watered garden, and like a spring of water, whose waters fail not.

Ps 25:9 ❙ THE MEEK WILL HE GUIDE in judgment: and the meek will he teach his way.

Ps 16:11 ❙ THOU WILT SHEW ME THE PATH OF LIFE: in thy presence is fulness of joy; at thy right hand there are pleasures for evermore.

Pr 3:5-6 ❙ Trust in the Lord with all thine heart; and lean not unto thine own understanding. In all thy ways acknowledge him, and he shall direct thy paths.

Ps 37:23 ❙ THE STEPS OF A GOOD MAN ARE ORDERED BY THE LORD: and he delighteth in his way.

CHRIST'S RIGHTEOUSNESS

Jer 23:6 ❙ In his days Judah shall be saved, and Israel shall dwell safely: and this is his name whereby he shall be called, THE LORD OUR RIGHTEOUSNESS.

Phil 1:11 ❙ Being filled with the fruits of righteousness, which are by Jesus Christ, unto the glory and praise of God.

Rom 3:22 ❙ Even the RIGHTEOUSNESS OF GOD WHICH IS BY FAITH OF JESUS CHRIST unto all and upon all them that believe: for there is no difference.

Rom 3:25 ❙ Whom God hath set forth to be a propitiation through faith in his blood, TO DECLARE HIS RIGHTEOUSNESS FOR THE REMISSION OF SINS that are past, through the forbearance of God.

Phil 3:9 ❙ And he found in him, not having mine own righteousness, which is of the law, but that which is through the faith of Christ, the RIGHTEOUSNESS WHICH IS OF GOD BY FAITH.

Rom 10:34 ❙ For they being ignorant of God's righteousness, and going about to establish their own righteousness, have not submitted themselves unto the righteousness of God. For CHRIST IS THE END OF THE LAW FOR RIGHTEOUSNESS to every one that believes.

1 Cor 1:30 ❙ But of him are ye in Christ Jesus, who of GOD IS MADE UNTO US wisdom, and RIGHTEOUSNESS, and sanctification, and redemption

Isa 54:17 ❙ No weapon that is formed against thee shall prosper; and every tongue that shall rise against thee in judgment thou shalt condemn. This is the heritage of the servants of the Lord, and THEIR RIGHTEOUSNESS IS OF ME, saith the Lord.

BLESSINGS OF THE FEAR OF THE LORD

Ps 147:11 ▎ THE LORD TAKETH PLEASURE in them that fear him, in those that hope in his mercy.

Ps 31:19-20 ▎ Oh how GREAT IS THY GOODNESS, which thou hast laid up for them that fear thee; which thou hast wrought for them that trust in thee before the sons of men! THOU SHALT HIDE them in the secret of thy presence FROM THE PRIDE OF MAN: thou shalt KEEP THEM secretly in a pavilion FROM THE STRIFE OF TONGUES.

Prov 3:7-8 ▎ Fear the Lord, and depart from evil. It shall be HEALTH TO THY NAVEL, and MARROW TO THY BONES.

Prov 1:7 ▎ The fear of the Lord is the BEGINNING OF KNOWLEDGE.

Mal 3:16-18 ▎ Then they that feared the Lord spake often one to another: and the Lord hearkened, and heard it, and a book of remembrance was written before him for them that feared the Lord, and that thought upon his name. And they shall be mine, saith the Lord of hosts, in that day when I make up my jewels; and I WILL SPARE THEM, as a man spareth his own son that serveth him. Then shall ye return, and discern between the righteous and the wicked, between him that serveth God and him that serveth him not.

Pro 1:31-33 ▎ Therefore shall they eat of the fruit of their own way, and be filled with their own devices. For the turning away of the simple shall slay them, and the prosperity of fools shall destroy them. But whoso hearkeneth unto me shall dwell safely, and shall be quiet from fear of evil.

Pro14:26 ❚ In the fear of the LORD is STRONG CONFIDENCE: and his children shall have a PLACE OF REFUGE.

Pro14:27 ❚ The fear of the LORD is a FOUNTAIN OF LIFE, to depart from the snares of death.

Mal 4:2 ❚ But unto you that fear my name shall the SUN OF RIGHTEOUSNESS arise with HEALING IN HIS WINGS.

Ps 25:12 ❚ What man is he that feareth the Lord? him SHALL HE TEACH in the way that he shall choose.

Ps 25:14 ❚ THE SECRET OF THE LORD is with them that fear him; and he will show them his covenant.

Ps 103:13 ❚ Like as a father pitieth his children, so THE LORD PITIETH them that fear him.

Luke 1:50 ❚ And HIS MERCY is on them that fear him from generation to generation.

THROUGH HIM

Rom 8:37 ▌ Nay, in all these things we are MORE THAN CONQUERORS THROUGH HIM that loved us.

Jn 3:17 ▌ For God sent not his Son into the world to condemn the world; but that the world THROUGH HIM might be SAVED.

Rom 5:9 ▌ Much more then being now justified by his blood, we shall be SAVED FROM WRATH THROUGH HIM.

1 Jn 4:9 ▌ In this was manifested the love of God toward us, because that God sent his only begotten Son into the world, that we might LIVE THROUGH HIM.

Jn 1:7 ▌ The same came for a witness, to bear witness of the Light, that all men THROUGH HIM might BELIEVE.

Jn 1:3 ▌ ALL THINGS WERE MADE THROUGH HIM and without him nothing was made that was made. (NKJV)

WITH HIM

Rom 6:4 ❙ Therefore we are BURIED WITH HIM by baptism into death: that like as Christ was raised up from the dead by the glory of the Father, even so we also should walk in newness of life.

Rom 6:6 ❙ Knowing this, that our old man is CRUCIFIED WITH HIM, that the body of sin might be destroyed, that henceforth we should not serve sin.

Rom 8:32 ❙ He that spared not his own Son, but delivered him up for us all, how shall he not WITH HIM also FREELY GIVE US ALL THINGS?

2 Cor 13:4 ❙ For though he was crucified through weakness, yet he liveth by the power of God. For we also are weak in him, but we shall LIVE WITH HIM by the power of God toward you.

Col 2:12 ❙ BURIED WITH HIM in baptism, wherein also ye are RISEN WITH HIM through the faith of the operation of God, who hath raised him from the dead.

Col 2:13-15 ❙ And YOU, being dead in your sins and the uncircumcision of your flesh, hath HE QUICKENED together WITH HIM, having forgiven you all trespasses; blotting out the handwriting of ordinances that was against us, which was contrary to us, and took it out of the way, nailing it to his cross; and having spoiled principalities and powers, he made a show of them openly, triumphing over them in it.

Col 3:4 ❙ When Christ, who is our life, shall appear, then SHALL YE ALSO APPEAR WITH HIM IN GLORY.

2 Tm 2:11 ▎ For if we BE DEAD WITH HIM, we shall also LIVE WITH HIM.

2 Tm 2:12 ▎ If we suffer, we shall also REIGN WITH HIM: if we deny him, he also will deny us.

1 Thess 5:10 ▎ Who died for us, that, whether we wake or sleep, we should LIVE TOGETHER WITH HIM.

IN HIM

Jn 1:4 ▌ IN HIM WAS LIFE; and the life was the light of men.

Phil 3:9 ▌ And BE FOUND IN HIM, not having mine own righteousness, which is of the law, but that which is through the faith of Christ, the righteousness which is of God by faith.

Col 1:19 ▌ For it pleased the Father that IN HIM SHOULD ALL FULNESS DWELL.

2 Cor 1:20 ▌ For all the PROMISES OF GOD IN HIM ARE YEA, and in him Amen, unto the glory of God by us.

2 Cor 5:21 ▌ For he hath made him to be sin for us, Who knew no sin; that we might be made the RIGHTEOUSNESS of God IN HIM.

2 Thess 1:12 ▌ That the name of our Lord Jesus Christ may be glorified in you, and ye in him, according to the grace of our God and the Lord Jesus Christ.

Col 2:6-7 ▌ As ye have therefore received Christ Jesus the Lord, so WALK YE IN HIM: rooted and built up in him, and stablished in the faith, as ye have been taught, abounding therein with thanksgiving.

Col 2:9 ▌ For IN HIM DWELLETH ALL THE FULNESS OF THE GODHEAD bodily.

Acts 10:43 ▌ Whosoever believeth IN HIM shall receive REMISSION OF SINS.

Acts 17:28 ▌ IN HIM we LIVE, and MOVE, and HAVE OUR BEING.

1 Jn 2:5 ▌ But whoso keepeth his word, in him verily is the LOVE OF GOD PERFECTED: hereby know we that we are IN HIM.

1 Jn 2:6 ▌ He that saith he ABIDETH IN HIM ought himself also so to walk, even as he walked.

1 Jn 2:8 ▌ Again, a new commandment I write unto you, which thing is true IN HIM and in you: because the DARKNESS IS PAST, and the true light now shineth.

Jn 3:3 ▌ And every man that hath this HOPE IN HIM purifieth himself, even as he is pure.

1 Jn 3:6 ▌ Whosoever abideth IN HIM sinneth not.

1 Jn 3:24 ▌ And he that keepeth His commandments dwelleth IN HIM, and He in him.

1 Jn 4:13 ▌ Hereby know we that we dwell IN HIM, and he in us, because he hath given us of his Spirit.

1 Jn 5:20 ▌ And we know that the Son of God is come, and hath given us an understanding, that we may know him that is true, and WE ARE IN HIM that is true.

1 Jn 5:14-15 ▌ And this is the CONFIDENCE that we have IN HIM, that if we ask any thing according to his will, he heareth us: And if we know that he hear us, whatsoever we ask, we know that we have the petitions that we desired of him.

1 Jn 3:5 ▌ And ye know that he was manifested to take away our sins; and IN HIM IS NO SIN.

Col 2:10 ▌ Ye are COMPLETE IN HIM, which is the head of all principality and power.

2 Sam 22:31 ▌ As for God, his way is perfect; the word of the LORD is tried: he is a buckler to all them that TRUST IN HIM.

Ps 37:5 ▌ Commit thy way unto the LORD; TRUST also IN HIM; and he shall bring it to pass.

1 Jn 1:5 ▌ God is light, and IN HIM IS NO DARKNESS at all.

Jn 3:16 ▌ Whosoever believeth IN HIM should not perish, but have EVERLASTING LIFE.

Pro 30:5 ▌ He is a SHIELD unto there that put their trust IN HIM.

Eph 1:4 ▌ He hath CHOSEN us IN HIM before the foundation of the world.

Jn 7:18 ▌ NO UNRIGHTEOUSNESS IS IN HIM.

Jn 13:31 ▌ GOD IS GLORIFIED IN HIM.

IN CHRIST JESUS

Rom 8:1 ▌ There is therefore now NO CONDEMNATION to them which are IN CHRIST JESUS, who walk not after the flesh, but after the Spirit.

Rom 3:24 ▌ Being justified freely by his grace through the REDEMPTION that is IN CHRIST JESUS.

Rom 8:2 ▌ For the law of the Spirit of life IN CHRIST JESUS hath made me FREE from the law of sin and death.

1 Cor 1:2 ▌ To them that are SANCTIFIED IN CHRIST JESUS, called to be saints.

1 Cor 1:30 ▌ But of him are ye IN CHRIST JESUS, who of God is made unto us WISDOM, and RIGHTEOUSNESS, and SANCTIFICATION, and REDEMPTION.

1 Cor 15:22 ▌ For as in Adam all die, even so IN CHRIST shall all be MADE ALIVE.

2 Cor 1:21 ▌ Now he which stablisheth us with you IN CHRIST, and hath ANOINTED us, is God.

2 Cor 2:14 ▌ Now thanks be unto God, which always calleth us to TRIUMPH IN CHRIST, and maketh manifest the savour of his knowledge by us in every place.

2 Cor 5:17 ▌ Therefore if any man be IN CHRIST, he is a NEW CREATURE: old things are passed away; behold, all things are become new.

Gal 2:4 ▌ Our LIBERTY which we have IN CHRIST JESUS.

Gal 3:28 ❚ There is neither Jew nor Greek, there is neither bond nor free, there is neither male nor female: for ye are ALL ONE IN CHRIST JESUS.

Eph 1:3 ❚ Blessed be the God and Father of our Lord Jesus Christ, who hath BLESSED US WITH ALL SPIRITUAL BLESSINGS in heavenly places IN CHRIST.

Eph 2:6 ❚ And hath RAISED US UP TOGETHER, and made us sit together IN HEAVENLY PLACES IN CHRIST JESUS.

Eph 2:10 ❚ For we are his WORKMANSHIP, CREATED IN CHRIST JESUS unto good works, which God hath before ordained that we should walk in them.

Rom 9:1 ❚ I say the TRUTH IN CHRIST, I lie not, my conscience also bearing me witness in the Holy Ghost.

Rom 8:38-39 ❚ For I am persuaded, that neither death, nor life, nor angels, nor principalities, nor powers, nor things present, nor things to come, nor height, nor depth, nor any other creature, shall be able to separate us from the LOVE OF GOD, which is IN CHRIST JESUS our Lord

Phil 3:3 ❚ For we are the circumcision, which worship God in the spirit, and REJOICE IN CHRIST JESUS, and have no confidence in the flesh.

Phil 3:14 ❚ I press toward the mark for the prize of the HIGH CALLING OF GOD IN CHRIST JESUS.

Eph 2:13 ❚ But now IN CHRIST JESUS ye who sometimes were far off are made nigh by the blood of Christ.

Eph 1:1-2 ❚ Paul, an apostle of Jesus Christ by the will of God, to the saints which are at Ephesus, and to the FAITHFUL

IN CHRIST JESUS: grace be to you, and peace, from God our Father, and from the Lord Jesus Christ.

1 Thess 5:18 ▍ In every thing give thanks: for this is the will of God IN CHRIST JESUS concerning you.

2 Tm 1:9 ▍ Who hath saved us, and CALLED US WITH AN HOLY CALLING, not according to our works, but according to his own purpose and grace, which was given us in Christ Jesus before the world began.

2 Tm 1:13 ▍ Hold fast the form of sound words, which thou hast heard of me, in FAITH AND LOVE which is IN CHRIST JESUS.

2 Tm 2:1 ▍ Thou therefore, my son, be strong in the GRACE that is IN CHRIST JESUS.

Gal 3:26 ▍ For ye are all the children of God by FAITH IN CHRIST JESUS.

Phlm 1:6 ▍ That the communication of thy faith may become effectual by the acknowledging of every good thing which is in you IN CHRIST JESUS.

1 Tm 1:14 ▍ And the grace of our Lord was exceeding abundant with FAITH AND LOVE which is IN CHRIST JESUS.

2 Tm 1:1 ▍ Paul, an apostle of Jesus Christ by the will of God, according to the PROMISE OF LIFE which is IN CHRIST JESUS.

2 Tm 2:10 ▍ Therefore I endure all things for the elect's sakes, that they may also obtain the SALVATION which is IN CHRIST JESUS with eternal glory.

2 Tm 3:12 ▍ Yea, and all that will live godly IN CHRIST

JESUS shall suffer persecution.

2 Tm 3:15 ▌ And that from a child thou hast known the holy scriptures, which are able to make thee wise unto salvation through FAITH which is IN CHRIST JESUS.

Section IV

Healing

God's Thoughts Concerning Healing

Prov 4: 20-22 ▍ Attend to my words; incline your ear to my sayings. Let them not depart from thine eyes; keep them in the midst of thine heart. For they are life to those that find them and health to all their flesh.

Health in the above verse means medicine, deliverance, curative, healing, and cure. Taken from Strong's concordance.

Isa 53:3-5 ▍ He is despised and rejected of men: a man of sorrows, and acquainted with grief: and we hid as it were our faces from him; he was despised, and we esteemed him not. Surely he hath borne our griefs, and carried our sorrows: yet we did esteem him stricken, smitten of God, and afflicted. But he was wounded for our transgressions, he was bruised for our iniquities; the chastisement for our peace was upon him; and with his stripes we are healed.

Jn 8:38 ▍ For I came down from heaven, not to do mine own will, but the will of him that sent me.

Jesus came to do his Father's will. Everything we see Jesus doing in the gospels was exactly what his Father wanted him to do. Matthew, an eyewitness to the miracles Jesus performed, gives the best translation and interpretation of Isaiah 53. He was there to experience it first hand. Matthew was fluent in the original Hebrew and Greek that the Bible was written in. Let's look at how he translated Isaiah 53.

Matt 8:16-17 ▌ When the even was come, they brought unto him many that were possessed with devils: and he cast out the spirits with his word, and healed all that were sick: that it might be fulfilled which was spoken by Esaias the prophet, saying, Himself took our infirmities, and bare our sicknesses.

Matt 9:20-22 ▌ And, behold, a woman which was diseased with an issue of blood twelve years came behind him, and touched the hem of his garment; For she said within herself, If I may but touch his garment, I shall be whole. But Jesus turned him about, and when he saw her, he said, Daughter be of good comfort; thy faith hath made thee whole. And the woman was made whole from that hour.

Matt 9: 28-29 ▌ And when he was come into the house, the blind men came to him: and Jesus saith unto them, Believe ye that I am able to do this? They said unto him, Yea, Lord. Then touched he their eyes, saying, According to your faith be it unto you.

Matt 9:35-36 ▌ And Jesus went about all the cities and villages, teaching in their synagogues, and preaching the gospel of the kingdom, and healing every sickness and every disease among the people. But when he saw the multitudes, he was moved with compassion on them, because they fainted, and were scattered abroad, as sheep having no shepherd.

Matt 10:1 ▌ And when he had called unto him his twelve disciples, he gave them power against unclean spirits, to cast them out; and to heal all manner sickness and all manner of disease.

Matt 12:15 ▌ Then the Pharisees went out, and held a council against him how they might destroy him. But when Jesus knew it, he withdrew himself from thence: and great multitudes followed him, and he healed them all.

Matt 13:15 ▌ For this people's heart is waxed gross, and their ears are dull of hearing, and their eyes they have closed; lest at any time they should see with their eyes, and hear with their ears, and should understand with their heart, and should be converted, and I should heal them.

Matt 14:14 ▌ And Jesus went forth, and saw a great multitude, and was moved with compassion toward their sick.

Matt 15:13 ▌ Every plant which my heavenly Father hath not planted shall be rooted up

Is cancer or any other disease something that God plants? If God does not plant it, then we have the right to expect it to be uprooted from our bodies.

Mark 2:17 ▌ When Jesus heard it, he saith unto them, They that are whole have no need of the physician, but they that are sick; I came not to call the righteous, but sinners to repentance.

What were the final instructions of Jesus to his disciples and the believer's that were yet to come?

Mark 16:15-18 ▌ Go ye into all the world, and preach the gospel to every creature. He that believeth and is baptized shall be saved; but he that believeth not shall be damned. And these signs shall follow them that believe, in my name shall they cast out devils; they shall speak with new tongues. They shall take up serpents; and if they drink any deadly thing, it shall not hurt them; they shall lay hands on the sick, and they shall recover.

Heb 13:8 ▌ Jesus Christ the same yesterday, today and forever.

If Jesus did only the things that please his Father, than healing must please God. Jesus was continually healing. Each healing Jesus administered was different. Some were healed as they went. Some were instantly healed. Some were given instructions to obey. When the little girl died, (Mark 5:22) her parents received instructions to give her something to eat. Why? Because she had been acutely ill and her body was weak. She needed to recover her strength and build up her body again. Some people were given instructions to repent and sin no more so that the sickness could not return. (Jn 5:14) Certain infirmities were only healed after the devil was cast out. (Mark 9:24) Some were leprous or maimed meaning they were missing body parts, but Jesus healed them all. (Matt 8:1) He was not a respecter of persons, but he did respect faith and respond to it. He also healed people because of the faith of others. (Matt 15:22)

The Bible contains countless examples of God healing and delivering people from all forms of sickness and evil. The following are just a small sample of the mighty works of God. I would encourage you to study the Bible on healing and deliverance for yourself and add to the list in this book. Then, help someone else get well.

Ex 15:26 ▌ If thou wilt diligently hearken to the voice of the Lord thy God, and wilt do that which is right in his sight, and wilt give ear to his commandments, and keep all his statutes, I will put none of these diseases upon thee, which I have brought upon the Egyptians: for I am the Lord that healeth thee.

Ps 30:2 ▌ O Lord my God, I cried unto thee, and thou hast healed me.

Mal 4:2 ▌ But unto you that fear my name shall the Sun of righteousness arise with healing in his wings.

Zech 13:1 ❙ In that day there shall be a fountain (the blood of Jesus) opened to the house of David and to the inhabitants of Jerusalem for sin and for uncleanness.

Many times in scripture uncleanness refers to sickness.

Ps 103:3 ❙ Who forgiveth all thine iniquities; who healeth all thy diseases.

Repentance from sin and healing often work together.

Ezek 18:21-22 ❙ But if a wicked man turns from all the sins he has committed and keeps all my decrees and does what is just and right, he will surely live; he will not die. None of the offenses he has committed will be remembered against him. Because of the righteous things he has done, he will live.

If God would do all this for the wicked, how much more his children?

Jer 33:6 ❙ Behold, I will bring it health and cure, I will cure them, and will reveal unto them the abundance of peace and truth.

Cure - a medicine, deliverance, healing, remedy, soundness, wholesome. (Strong's concordance)

Rom 8:11 ❙ But if the Spirit of him that raised up Jesus from the dead dwell in you, he that raised up Christ from the dead shall also quicken your mortal bodies by his Spirit that dwelleth in you.

Quicken - vitalize, make alive, give, give life to (to endue with life, life in the absolute sense as God has it) that which the Father has in himself, Resurrection life. (Strong's concordance, Vine's Dictionary)

James 5:14-16 ❙ Is any sick among you? Let him call for the elders of the church; and let them pray over him, anointing him with oil in the name of the Lord: and the prayer of faith shall save the sick, and the Lord shall raise him up; and if he hath committed sins, they shall be forgiven him. Confess your faults one to another, and pray one for another, that ye may be healed. The effectual fervent prayer of a righteous man availeth much.

Why would Jesus command us to do something, and then not give us the power or ability to do it?

Section V

To Be Born Again

The Power of the Cross

Isa 53:1-6 NKJ ▮ Who has believed our report? And to whom has the arm of the Lord been revealed? For He shall grow up before Him as a tender plant, And as a root out of dry ground. He has no form or comeliness; and when we see Him, There is no beauty that we should desire Him. He is despised and rejected by men. A man of sorrows and acquainted with grief. And we hid, as it were, our faces from Him; He was despised, and we did not esteem Him. Surely He has borne our griefs and carried our sorrows; yet we esteemed Him stricken, Smitten by God, and afflicted. But He was wounded for our transgressions; He was bruised for our iniquities: The chastisement for our peace was upon Him, and by His stripes we are healed. All we like sheep have gone astray; we have turned, every one, to his own way; and the Lord has laid on Him the iniquity of us all.

Col 2:13-15 NKJ ▮ And you, being dead in your trespasses and the uncircumcision of you flesh, He has made alive together with Him, having forgiven you all trespasses, having wiped out the handwriting of requirements that was against us, which was contrary to us. And He has taken it out of the way, having nailed it to the cross. Having disarmed principalities and powers, He made a public spectacle of them, triumphing over them in it.

Heb 12:2 NLT ▮ We do this by keeping our eyes on Jesus, the champion who initiates and perfects our faith. Because of the joy awaiting Him, He endured the cross, disregarding its shame. Now He is seated in the place of honor beside God's throne.

Ro 10:9-10 KJ ▮ If you confess with your mouth the Lord Jesus and believe in your heart that God has raised him from the dead, you will be saved. For with the heart one believes unto righteousness, and with the mouth confession is made unto salvation.

1 Cor 2:8-9 KJ ▮ Which none of the princes of this world knew: for had thy known it, they would not have crucified the Lord of glory. But as it is written, Eye hath not seen, nor ear heard, neither have entered into the heart of man, the things which God hath prepared for them that love him.

Phil 2:8-10 KJ ▮ And being found in fashion as a man, he humbled himself, and became obedient unto death, even the death of the cross. Wherefore God also hath highly exalted him, and given him a name which is above every name: That at the name of Jesus every knee should bow, of things in heaven, and things in earth, and things under the earth.

1 Cor 1:18 KJ ▮ For the preaching of the cross is to them that perish foolishness; but unto us which are saved it is the power of God.

Eph 2:14-16 KJ ▮ For he is our peace, who hath made both one, and hath broken down the middle wall of partition between us; Having abolished in his flesh the enmity, even the law of commandments contained in ordinances; for to make in himself of twain one new man, so making peace; And that he might reconcile both unto God in one body by the cross, having slain the enmity thereby.

Gal 3:13-14 NKJ ▮ Christ has redeemed us from the curse of the law, having become a curse for us (for it is written, Cursed is everyone who hangs on a tree) that the blessing of Abraham might come upon the Gentiles in Christ Jesus, that we might receive the promise of the Spirit through faith.

What God Wants You to Receive

Jn 1:12 ▮ But as many as received him, to them gave he power to become the sons of God, even to them that believe on his name.

Jn 11:25-26 ▮ Jesus said unto her, I am the resurrection, and the life: he that believeth in me, though he were dead, yet shall he live: And whosoever liveth and believeth in me shall never die. Believest thou this?

Acts 26:18 ▮ To open their eyes, and to turn them from darkness to light, and from the power of Satan unto God, that they may receive forgiveness of sins, and inheritance among them which are sanctified by faith that is in me.

Amos 5:4 ▮ For thus saith the Lord unto the house of Israel, Seek ye me, and ye shall live.

Prov 24:4-5 ▮ And by knowledge shall the chambers be filled with all precious and pleasant riches. A wise man is strong; yea, a man of knowledge increaseth strength.

Prov 28:10 ▮ He who leads the upright along an evil path will fall into his own trap, but the blameless will receive a good inheritance.

Matt 11:5 ▮ The blind receive their sight, and the lame walk, the lepers are cleansed, and the deaf hear, the dead are raised up, and the poor have the gospel preached to them.

Rom 5:17 ▮ For if, by the trespass of the one man, death reigned through that one man, how much more will those who receive God's abundant provision of grace and of the gift of righteousness reign in life through the one man, Jesus Christ.

Isa 61:7 ▌ For your shame ye shall have double; and for confusion they shall rejoice in their portion: therefore in their land they shall possess the double: everlasting joy shall be unto them.

Matt 11:5 ▌ The blind receive their sight, and the lame walk, the lepers are cleansed, and the deaf hear, the dead are raised up, and the poor have the gospel preached to them.

Rom 5:17 ▌ For if, by the trespass of the one man, death reigned through that one man, how much more will those who receive God's abundant provision of grace and of the gift of righteousness reign in life through the one man, Jesus Christ.

Matt 19:29 ▌ And every one that hath forsaken houses, or brethren, or sisters, or father, or mother, or wife, or children, or lands, for my name's sake, shall receive an hundredfold, and shall inherit everlasting life.

Heb 4:16 ▌ Let us then approach the throne of grace with confidence, so that we may receive mercy and find grace to help us in our time of need.

Matt 21:21 ▌ Jesus answered and said unto them, Verily I say unto you, If ye have faith, and doubt not, ye shall not only do this which is done to the fig tree, but also if ye shall say unto this mountain, Be thou removed, and be thou cast into the sea; it shall be done.

2 Cor 6:1-2 ▌ As God's fellow workers we urge you not to receive God's grace in vain. For he says, "In the time of my favor I heard you, and in the day of salvation I helped you."

I tell you, now is the time of God's favor, now is the day of salvation.

Mark 10:15 ▌ Verily I say unto you, whosoever shall not receive the kingdom of God as a little child, he shall not enter therein.

1 Tm 1:16 ▌ For that very reason I was shown mercy so that in me, the worst of sinners, Christ Jesus might display his unlimited patience as an example for those who would believe on him and receive eternal life.

Mark 11:22-26 ▌ And Jesus answering saith unto them, Have faith in God. For verily I say unto you, that whosoever shall say unto this mountain, Be thou removed, and be thou cast into the sea; and shall not doubt in his heart, but shall believe that those things which he saith shall come to pass; he shall have whatsoever he saith. Therefore I say unto you, what things soever ye desire, when ye pray, believe that ye receive them, and ye shall have them. And when ye stand praying, forgive, if ye have ought against any: that your Father also which is in heaven may forgive you your trespasses. But if ye do not forgive, neither will your Father which is in heaven forgive your trespasses.

Luke 18:40-41 ▌ Jesus stopped and ordered the man to be brought to him. When he came near, Jesus asked him, "What do you want me to do for you?" "Lord, I want to see," he replied.

Jn 16:24 ▌ Hitherto have ye asked nothing in my name: ask, and ye shall receive, that your joy may be full.

Gal 3:13-14 ▌ Christ hath redeemed us from the curse of the law, being made a curse for us: for it is written, Cursed is every one that hangeth on a tree: That the blessing of

Abraham might come on the Gentiles through Jesus Christ; that we might receive the promise of the Spirit through faith.

Acts 1:8 ▌ But ye shall receive power, after that the Holy Ghost is come upon you: and ye shall be witnesses unto me both in Jerusalem, and in all Judea, and in Samaria, and unto the uttermost part of the earth.

Heb 10:35-36 ▌ Cast not away therefore your confidence, which hath great recompence of reward. For ye have need of patience, that, after ye have done the will of God, ye might receive the promise.

James 1:12 ▌ Blessed is the man that endureth temptation: for when he is tried, he shall receive the crown of life, which the Lord hath promised to them that love him.

TO BE BORN AGAIN

Heb 3:20 Behold, I stand at the door, and knock: if any man hear my voice, and open the door, I will come in to him, and will sup with him and he with me.

Rom 10:9-10 That if thou shalt confess with thy mouth the Lord Jesus, and shalt believe in thine heart that God hath raised him from the dead, thou shalt be saved. For with the heart man believeth unto righteousness; and with the mouth confession is made unto salvation.

Jesus, I believe you died for my sins, I believe you rose from the dead. I confess you as my Lord and Savior. Please come into my life and make me your child. I confess my sins to you. Help me to know what is pleasing to you. Give me the power to turn away from all sin. I promise to live my life for you. Thank you for writing my name in the Lamb's Book of Life. If you've prayed this prayer for the first time, let someone else know. If you've rededicated your life to the Lord, know he is the God of a second chance. His Word tells us his mercies are new every morning. Please write to me and let me know. I encourage you to join a local church that believes the Bible is the Word of God.

Ask the Lord to direct your steps.

He won't disappoint you!

SUSAN EAVES

Inspirational Keynote Speaker

Susan Eaves is a teacher, author and personal growth coach.

Her life has been described as truly inspiring. She has overcome panic attacks, severe depression, tragedy and a heart-breaking past. She teaches with joy, compassion, humor and mesmerizing motivation.

Is your group or organization looking for someone that can captivate an audience with life-changing insights and real life examples? Susan inspires people from all walks of life with God-given strategies that work! She shares the life-changing principles that God taught her in the valley. These principles changed her life and have helped change the lives of many others.

For over twenty-three years she has taught her life enrichment principles at business conferences, seminars, and churches internationally.

Susan has been a guest on a multitude of television and radio shows.

Her passion is people. Her message - God can turn around the most desperate, unfair, hopeless, heart-breaking circumstances and bring destiny and purpose to them.

Be inspired as Susan shares how to overcoming toxic thinking, recover from tragedy and devastation, and go on to lead a fulfilling and victorious life.

IN SUSAN'S OWN WORDS:

I know that God has put me here to help others come out of devastation and to break the cycles of hopelessness and defeat. What God has done in my life, he wants to do in the lives of others. My assignment and joy is to show others how...

A Sample of Susan's Life Changing Topics

Give God One Year, Transform Your Life Forever
Rediscovering Purpose after Life-Shattering Events
Defeating Toxic Thinking
Overcoming Adversity
Triumphing over Panic Attacks, Anxiety and Stress
Victory over Depression
Forgiving the Impossible

For contact or additional information visit our websites.
susaneaves.com
theiambook.com
thecrisisbible.com
goodfellasofthebible.com
overcominglearningdisabilities.com

Or write us at:
Good Fellas Publishing
P.O. Box 7
Osprey, FL 34229

www.ingramcontent.com/pod-product-compliance
Lightning Source LLC
Chambersburg PA
CBHW051822090426
42736CB00011B/1611